1967

P9-AOM-340

Warner
Agrarian conditions in modern

3 0301 00022790 6

This book may be kept

FOURTEEN DAYS

1966

AGRARIAN CONDITIONS
IN
MODERN EUROPEAN HISTORY

MAIN THEMES IN EUROPEAN HISTORY

Bruce Mazlish, General Editor

AGRARIAN CONDITIONS

IN

MODERN EUROPEAN HISTORY

Edited by

CHARLES K. WARNER

343

LIBRARY
College of St. Francis
JOLIET, ILL.

THE MACMILLAN COMPANY, NEW YORK
COLLIER-MACMILLAN LIMITED, LONDON

© Copyright, Charles Warner, 1966

All rights reserved. No part of this book may be reproduced or utilized in any form or by any means, electronic or mechanical, including photocopying, recording or by any information storage and retrieval system, without permission in writing from the Publisher.

First Printing

Library of Congress catalog card number: 66–17875

THE MACMILLAN COMPANY, NEW YORK
COLLIER-MACMILLAN CANADA, LTD., TORONTO, ONTARIO

PRINTED IN THE UNITED STATES OF AMERICA

630.94
9t279

FOREWORD

History, we are frequently told, is a seamless web. However, by isolating and studying the strands that compose the tapestry of man's past, we are able to discern the pattern, or patterns, of which it is comprised. Such an effort does not preclude a grasp of the warp and woof, and the interplay of the strands; rather, it eventually demands and facilitates such a comprehension. It is with this in mind that the individual volumes of the MAIN THEMES series have been conceived.

The student will discover, for example, that the population changes discussed in one volume relate to the changes in technology traced in another volume; that both changes are affected by, and affect in turn, religious and intellectual developments; and that all of these changes and many more ramify into a complicated historical network through all the volumes. In following through this complex interrelationship of the parts, the student recreates for himself the unity of history.

Each volume achieves its purpose, and its appeal to a general audience, by presenting the best articles by experts in the field of history and allied disciplines. In a number of cases, the articles have been translated into English for the first time. The individual volume editor has linked these contributions into an integrated account of his theme, and supplied a selected bibliography by means of footnotes for the student who wishes to pursue the topic further. The introduction is an original treatment of the problems in the particular field. It provides continuity and background for the articles, points out gaps in the existing literature, offers new interpretations, and suggests further research.

The volumes in this series afford the student of history an unusual opportunity to explore subjects either not treated or touched upon lightly in a survey text. Some examples are population—the dramatis personae of history; war—the way of waging peace by other means; the rise of technology and science in relation to society; the role of religious

40569

and cultural ideas and institutions; the continuous ebb and flow of exploration and colonialism; and the political and economic works contrived by modern man. Holding fast to these Ariadne threads, the student penetrates the fascinating labyrinth of history.

BRUCE MAZLISH
General Editor

CONTENTS

AGRARIAN CONDITIONS
IN
MODERN EUROPEAN HISTORY

INTRODUCTION

Only for a brief moment in history and in a few places on earth have men known anything but an agrarian environment.

A. Whitney Griswold, *Farming and Democracy*

I

It is a commonplace that, if man cannot live by bread alone, he also cannot exist without it. Yet only a small part of the accumulated labors of historians has been devoted to describing how and under what conditions men have worked to procure a living from the soil. For an explanation of the relative neglect of a record "by the side of which," as Frederick Jackson Turner once wrote, "much that has passed as history is the merest frippery," [1] the reader should study the changing fashions in historiography. Only a few general observations can be offered here on some of the influences that have affected the writing of agrarian history.

There has been the indifference reserved for the familiar. In the middle of the nineteenth century, when history came into its own as an academic discipline, Europe (and America) constituted an agrarian society in the sense that agriculture was still the chief source of livelihood for the greatest number of people. Change, however, pointed in the direction of an urbanized and industrial society. And to the extent that historians in the nineteenth and early twentieth century abandoned their overriding concern with political history in order to look at the economic sphere, they turned mostly to the history of trade, industry, and finance. Moreover, all these subjects adapted themselves quite conveniently to the prevailing idea of progress.

Agriculture was more difficult to fit in. True, an Agricultural Revolution was propounded as a sort of country cousin to the Industrial Revolution. But apart from this change and a few others, the historian saw the fields and their inhabitants, if he looked at them at all, as governed by a more timeless and therefore less interesting order than that in force at the seats of power. His indifference was further bolstered by the relative scarceness of sources for agrarian history. The tillers of the soil, for obvious reasons, have been the least articulate

[1] "The Significance of History," *The Early Writings of Frederick Jackson Turner* (Madison: The University of Wisconsin Press, 1938), p. 48.

I

members of society when it comes to leaving a written record of their past.

Today it is hard to imagine that most historians would be indifferent to agrarian history because of a too great familiarity with farming. If they come to ignore it, the cause would appear to lie in the opposite direction. One American historian has worried that life and education in artificial surroundings may make it difficult for future historians "to succeed in recovering imaginatively what the old milieu of thousands of years was like." [2] Contrariwise, another believes that agricultural history will have a flourishing revival through "interest associated with the unknown and judgment which comes through perspective and the passing of time." [3]

We may hope for the second alternative, but whatever dangers or advantages the future may hold for the study of agrarian history, historians are turning to it in increasing numbers. In a matter of decades, professional societies, institutes, and journals have been founded. This has been particularly true in Western Europe, which though heavily urbanized and industrialized is still so intensively farmed that tangible evidence of the agrarian past is less dissipated in space or time than in our own country. There a growing number of scholars have turned to long-neglected local archives, estate records, and the like. Where the written record fails, such sophisticated techniques as carbon dating and pollen and soil analyses have been used at excavations. Recently, in England, aerial surveys have located the sites of villages and fields lost to enclosure.

Of equal importance for the future of agrarian history, however, are some of the tendencies developing within the historical discipline as a whole. As historians have become more aware of the methods and contributions of sociology, demography, anthropology, and geography, and as comparative studies have opened up an area of valuable collaboration between historians and students of these disciplines, history has been increasingly interpreted in terms of social and physical environment. As a result, more account has been taken of agrarian conditions in historical studies not exclusively concerned with them. The agrarian environment has been seen as an active as well as a passive force in historical development. Agrarian history, in short, has moved or, at

[2] Carl Bridenbaugh, "The Great Mutation," *American Historical Review*, LXVIII (January, 1963), p. 319.

[3] Gilbert C. Fite, "Expanded Frontiers in Agricultural History," *Agricultural History*, XXV (October, 1961), p. 179.

least, has begun to move into a position more compatible with the truth contained in the quotation at the head of this Introduction. In keeping with this trend, the selections which follow are intended to give some idea of the important influence that agrarian conditions have had on European history in general, at the same time touching in chronological sequence on some of the major aspects of Europe's agricultural development.

II

A distinguished agrarian historian has recently written that "research in the field of agricultural history in the various West European countries has not yet reached the stage where one can proceed to a synthesis of the subject." [4] This will be taken as a statement of despair only by those who like their progress to be in a straight line. Current research reveals a fascinating combination of continuity and change in European agriculture, far more complex than previously suspected. As has been the case in other branches of history, neat generalizations like the Agricultural Revolution have become blurred at the edges, if indeed they are not ready to be scrapped.

Thus alternate husbandry, traditionally identified with the agrarian reformers of the eighteenth century, was practiced in the seventeenth, not only in Norfolk, its reputed center of origin, but in several other regions of England as well. As early as the sixteenth century, some parts of the Netherlands were importing grain from abroad and supplying cities with the products of an intensive and specialized agriculture. During the late Middle Ages crop rotations could be found in the Low Countries that were not too dissimilar from those more commonly associated with the seventeenth and eighteenth centuries.

On the other hand, in areas adjoining those where more sophisticated rotations might be in force, the majority of Dutch cultivators were probably leaving a field fallow one year out of every three. In England the enclosure of open fields was supposed to have destroyed the yeomanry, but at Caythorpe in Lincolnshire it is possible that there were more freeholders at the middle of the nineteenth century than at the beginning of the seventeenth. In late nineteenth-century France cattle were still to be seen enjoying the right of common pasture in the stubble fields, just as they had in the Middle Ages.

[4] B. H. Slicher van Bath, *The Agrarian History of Western Europe* A.D. 500–1850 (New York: St. Martin's Press, 1963), p. vii.

From these examples among others to be found in the selections that follow it may be seen that the course of change is a central problem in agricultural history. Quite properly, agrarian historians have been concerned to fix with more accuracy than in the past the time and place of the introduction of new techniques. It is possible that these investigations will bring forth new causal explanations for technological change, though there are so many concomitants for this that probably no simple explanation will ever be possible.

With this proviso in mind, it may be remarked that in the Middle Ages the course of agricultural progress seems most clearly evident in the reciprocal relationship between improved farming techniques and the formation of urban centers. With the growth of the latter the influence of the market becomes more direct. The dramatic switch from arable to sheep farming in the fifteenth and sixteenth centuries, for example, is a clear case of change for economic advantage. In the succeeding centuries it is perhaps not too great a generalization to say that economic factors have increasingly influenced land use and patterns of landholding and have helped provide the environment for the technological revolution in agriculture, which has continued to our day.

That economic factors are in the forefront of current research is abundantly illustrated by many of the selections in this volume. But economic factors do not of themselves explain the sharp contrasts between change and continuity noted in the examples above.. As G. E. Mingay suggests in his reconsideration of the Agricultural Revolution included here, earlier historians were too ready to attribute regional survivals of older forms of agriculture to "the obtuse conservatism of the farmers." More recently, the study of historical geography has changed such verdicts to a large extent by bringing into consideration soils and other topographic factors which limited possibilities for the adoption of new techniques. But it seems that some place must be given to social attitudes in any study of European agriculture. Too often, when all other factors have been more or less equal, uneconomic crops and archaic practices will still be found existing side by side with newer forms of agriculture.

III

The selections in this volume are so arranged that the reader can trace the themes of change and continuity across the modern era. A few words of guidance, however, are in order, especially for the American reader. The latter should disabuse himself of the notion that the peasant is necessarily a wretched individual practicing a primitive agriculture. This could be an accurate description of most peasants for long periods of history. But there have always been well-to-do peasants, and today, as for some time past, the essential difference between an American farmer and a European peasant is their attitude towards the land. Briefly, to the American, land is an asset in a capitalistic enterprise to be exchanged like any other when the opportunity for profit warrants it. To the peasant, it is a heritage received from his ancestors, to be guarded, added to, if possible, and passed on to his children. This attitude reinforces and is reinforced by strong feelings of community and place. And closely related to these feelings is the inherited experience of centuries when agriculture was a collective enterprise.

Thus our first selection (Homans) takes us back to the Middle Ages and a description of the open-field village system. This system is more than just a convenient starting point for a survey of the process of change. Its communal organization of agriculture was the framework against which agricultural innovators had to push until they succeeded in breaking it in the eighteenth century. The beginnings of this pressure can be seen in the rise of intensive husbandry in the Netherlands (Slicher van Bath).

The new farming techniques introduced there could be and were practiced in the open fields. But the collective restraints of the open-field system meant, in effect, that new techniques had to be adopted by all villagers or none. How, for example, could one man plant root crops on his strips of the fallow if his neighbors insisted on their right of pasture in the same field? Indeed, what great profit was there even in keeping strips free from weeds if your neighbor neglected his? Thus some of the enclosed plots found in the open fields during the Middle Ages may have been due to a desire to improve techniques, and the long struggle was begun then for what Marc Bloch has so appropriately called "agrarian individualism."

The first real break, however, in the open-field system was made by enclosures for sheep raising in fifteenth- and sixteenth-century England (Beresford). As has been suggested earlier, these enclosures had little to do with new techniques but represented chiefly the exchange of one type of farming for another, motivated by a shift in the relative prices of grain and wool. These enclosures are important for the course we are tracing here because of the precedent they set, penalties notwithstanding, and because alarm over the resulting rural depopulation shows more than a trace of social conservatism.

Formerly, interest in enclosures was centered on the Tudor period and the eighteenth-century Agricultural Revolution. We now know that a good deal of enclosure for sheep raising must have occurred before the Tudors (Beresford) and that the later enclosures for improved farming date back to the seventeenth century (Hosford, Mingay). By that century a degree of social acceptance for the process might be indicated by comparing the enclosers of Caythorpe, men moved "chiefly by a prospect of improving their estates" (Hosford), with the "unreasonable covetous persons" who enclosed for sheep farming (Beresford). Certainly the enclosure at Caythorpe caused relatively little social dislocation. But resistance to change there is still reflected in the tortuous litigation preceding enclosure and the lord of the manor's belief that it was unlucky to enclose.

At all events, enclosure continued during the eighteenth century at an accelerated pace, greatly aided by Acts of Parliament, until by the first decades of the nineteenth century open fields and commons had all but disappeared from the English landscape. That this was accomplished with less disruption of traditional farming systems and landholding structures than earlier historians believed is pointed out in Mingay's reconsideration of the Agricultural Revolution.

In France, during the eighteenth century, there was a good deal of official enthusiasm for agriculture inspired by Physiocratic doctrines and some administrative encouragement of agricultural improvements including enclosure (Lefebvre). But because many landowners preferred to continue to collect rents and feudal dues rather than farm and because there was a massive class of small peasants avid for available land for whom collective rights such as common pasture were vital for survival, the progress of enclosure was negligible in comparison with England. The French Revolution, by abolishing feudal rights and dues, removed the legal hindrances to enclosure, and the sale of confiscated lands offered the peasants the opportunity, at least, of increasing their holdings. But these measures were not enough to satisfy the peasants' land hunger, and so the mass of the peasantry pressed for the maintenance or revival of the old collective rights. In addition, the practical impossibility of reallocating the scattered strips of peasant holdings by decree virtually required the continuance of the collective restraints of the open-field system long after they were legally abolished (Bloch). These circumstances go far towards explaining the markedly traditional character of much of French agriculture until our own day.

The French experience, however, was not wholly unique. In fact, by the mid-nineteenth century the way in which the agriculture of each nation had broken out of the collective feudal pattern, in combination with the general effects of economic progress, had in large measure determined the character of all West European agriculture, England included (Tracy). The establishment of agrarian individualism saw England, with a longer experience of enclosure and industrialization, moving towards larger and more efficient farms. France, industrializing more slowly, seemed to be becoming a nation of small peasant proprietors. Other countries leaned towards one or the other of these lines of development.

Although the element of continuity thus remained strong, the forces making for change assumed new dimensions after the middle of the century. The rise of urban industry and the parallel growth of cities intensified the relationship between the agricultural and urban sectors of the economy. The application of science and mechanics to agriculture so quickened the pace of progress in the second half of the nineteenth century that this period might more aptly be called the Agricultural Revolution. But the change that affected the majority of farmers most directly was the invasion of the European market by cheaper American grain.

As Tracy explains, this competition brought on an agricultural depression in all West European countries, an adaptation to changed circumstances in some, and a defensive reaction in the form of tariffs in others. Adaptation made economic sense, but tariffs could be additionally justified on grounds both of national self-sufficiency and the social benefits of preserving the rural population and its way of life.

It must be emphasized, however, that neither of these approaches could solve all the problems of agriculture, which in the course of the twentieth century became acute and general. The chief difficulty was that, in an industrialized society, agriculture, in spite of production gains, saw its share of the national income shrinking disproportionately. This was reflected in the generally lower standard of living of the rural population and the "price scissors" the farmer found himself caught in when he attempted to buy needed equipment. One solution might have been a rationalization of agriculture which would have eliminated the inefficient farm and brought the per capita output of agriculture more in line with that of industry. But while some part of government policy aimed at a degree of rationalization, the ballot box set practical limits to the elimination of the marginal producer.

Thus, increasing government intervention in the production and marketing of agricultural goods, a significant development of the years between the wars, took the form of palliative measures which could only hope to ease, rather than insure, the adjustment of agriculture to an industrial age. In countries where tariff protection had been adopted and there was a numerous small peasant class—France is a good example—the path of adjustment was particularly difficult. The type of protection that shielded the peasantry from competition tended to insulate it from change. The result was that an important segment of the rural population, economically and socially deprived and turned in on itself, remained suspicious of new ways. Peasants, in many instances, were incapable of taking advantage of such government help as credit or technical assistance that would have been of immediate benefit to them.

It could not be expected, however, that the peasantry of an advanced industrial democracy would remain forever impervious to outside influences. Army service, some political experience, reports by villagers returning from better-paying jobs in the city, improved transportation facilities, better schooling, an increased volume of communications media—these have all influenced the peasants towards an acceptance of new ideas and a desire to better their lot. This has been particularly true of the past several decades. The two sketches (Wright) which form the concluding selection of this book show how the winds of change are blowing today in the most traditionally conservative section of French society.

In almost every respect, such as landholding patterns, technical progress, or status of the peasantry, the course of agrarian history in East Europe (although we shall deal only with Russia as an example) offers notable contrasts with that of lands to the west. Thus, during the fifteenth and sixteenth centuries, when in Western Europe labor services and other manorial impositions were being commuted into cash payments or falling into disuse, manorialism was just becoming established in Russia. In ensuing centuries the bonds of serfdom were tightened rather than relaxed. Catherine the Great was considered an enlightened monarch by the eighteenth-century *philosophes* and professed great interest in agriculture. But she presided over a nation where a greater part of the population were subjected to a more debasing type of serfdom than had ever been the case in medieval England or France. By the mid-nineteenth century, when agrarian individualism had won the day in the West, the open-field system was still universal in Russia. Agricultural equipment was primitive in the extreme, and fallowing was widely practiced.

In 1861 serfdom was abolished, but it was a reform that miscarried (Volin). The best lands remained in the hands of the big estate owners and peasant holdings were often insufficient for a living, so that peasants remained economically dependent on the neighboring landlord. Further, the regulations by which land was allotted to the peasants through the *mir* or village community perpetuated some of the civil and landholding disabilities of serfdom. These were abolished by 1907, but the need for agrarian reform remained insistent up to to the eve of the 1917 Revolution. In November of that year, peasant land hunger was appeased by partition of the estates, one of the first acts of the new Bolshevik government. The following year, however, nationalization of the land was proclaimed. And within little more than a decade the peasants found themselves being dragooned into collective farms, where, with some concessions, they have remained to the present (Volin).

There is, perhaps, a tenuous continuity in Russia between the communal agriculture of the *mir* and today's *kolkhoz*. But peasant revolts for land and freedom in every century since the seventeenth, and most recently the terrible expenditure of human lives in liquidating the *kulaks,* suggest what the real aspirations of the Russian peasants have always been. History in the subjunctive is rarely profitable. It is at least worth surmising, however, that if Peter the Great had extended his forced modernization tactics from Russian industry to Russian agriculture, if Catherine the Great had liberated the serfs, and if Nicholas II had permitted an agrarian and political democracy, Russia's agrarian development might not have been too different in its fundamentals from that of France. But Catherine had to depend on her landholding nobility for governing, and by Nicholas's time autocracy had become a principle to be defended at all costs. The greatest of these costs, as it turned out, was disregarding the peasants' legitimate desire for land and political equality. Change, when it came, came forcibly and from above, and ultimately the peasants' desires were again disregarded. Under the Tsars and the Soviets the more normal course of agrarian evolution seems to have been sacrificed both to ideology and to expediency.

IV

In conclusion, a few words may be offered on the important role of agrarian conditions in a full understanding of European history in general. Whether agrarian conditions are interpreted solely in terms of land division and forms of occupancy or in a wider sense of including agricultural techniques, prices, crops, and the like, their influence has been immense. This is not to say that it has been obvious. An enormous effort of historical imagination is still required to understand what a peasant's life was like in the Middle Ages. And consequently to realize what seemingly simple innovations such as the three-field system or the horse-collar meant in terms of food and work saved. Yet it is advances in agriculture that, by their liberation of men from the tyranny of the soil, have made possible the increasing division of tasks on which our society and history rest.

Besides being a concomitant of material and cultural progress, agrarian conditions have played an important role in shaping political institutions. Feudalism, for example, only becomes comprehensible as a system adapted to governing an agrarian society of scattered self-sufficient units. On the other hand, as will be noted later (Homans), the open-field system required a considerable amount of local self-government which was carried over into the towns. Is it too much to say that the communal decisions and egalitarian aspects of the open-field village allowed a tradition of democracy to develop? Or that enclosures contributed to the ascendancy of the gentry in Parliament? Can it be denied that in both the French and Russian Revolutions agrarian and constitutional reforms were closely linked?

This line of questioning can be extended further. What is the connection, for example, between the rise of intensive husbandry in the Low Countries and that area's early commercial preeminence? And, by the same token, to what extent did Spain's favoring sheep raising over arable farming (Klein) contribute to her spectacular economic decline in the seventeenth century? Did enclosures, by furnishing the manpower, stimulate England's Industrial Revolution and overseas expansion? (This is debatable, but enclosures must at least have helped the process.) Was France's relatively slower industrialization attributable to the fact that peasant property was in practice, if not in principle, firmly established before the Revolution? And how has this affected her subsequent history? As can be demonstrated, forms of landholding have a direct influence on social attitudes. And these, it can be argued, determine political and economic behavior to a large degree. There are, of course, no monocausal factors in historical change. But the range of these few questions suggests the importance of agrarian conditions as a strand in the seamless web of history.

MEN AND THE LAND IN THE
MIDDLE AGES*

George C. Homans

George C. Homans is Professor of Social Relations at Harvard University. A sociologist who has written widely on Anglo-Saxon and medieval England, he is representative of the interdisciplinary approach that agrarian history encourages. Historians of an earlier generation tended to see the open-field villages as communities that developed according to preconceived notions of justice and political order. For Homans, "the village was what it was because the villagers worked together," and the persistence of the open-field system is better understood by explaining its social utility than by concentrating on its economic inefficiency.

I

To find out what any ancient society was like, students must look at landscapes, for the peoples who know the plow and the cultivation of cereals leave their characteristic marks upon the land they occupy, and these may well be their most enduring memorial, just as the stone walls they built are likely to be the most enduring memorial of the invasion of New England by the English. Long after the blood lines of a society have died out or the society itself has changed its ways, by the surface of fields, their shape, and the distribution of the old house sites may be read the traditional arrangements by which the society made its living: the agricultural techniques people had at their command and the ways in which they grouped themselves and worked together in using these techniques. Furthermore, these traditional ways of making a living are in a relation of mutual dependence with the other customs of the society, so that the study of landscapes which are not

* Reprinted, by permission, from SPECULUM XI, 3 (July 1936), published by the Mediaeval Academy of America.

natural but made by men is more than the study of different farming practices. It is the study of societies insofar as they are determined by and determine their use of the land.

The people of Europe in the Middle Ages were busy, almost wholly, with tilling the soil; therefore a study of mediaeval landscape is a good beginning for the study of mediaeval society. And it is no more nonsense to talk about mediaeval landscape than it is to talk about mediaeval art, for in many parts of Europe we can still look at mediaeval landscapes just as we can still look at cathedrals. Indeed, the landscapes are older than the cathedrals, for they are the engraving of societies which were in their prime when written history begins. Four hundred years ago, when people first began to take an interest in such matters, the lines were even clearer, and at that time observers made a distinction between two main kinds of English countryside, which they called *champion* and *woodland*. *Champion* country—the word comes from the French *campagne*—was the country of great open stretches of arable fields broken only, here and there, by stands of trees and by the buildings of the villages each clustered around the spire of the parish church. *Woodland* country did not always mean what we mean by woodland, that is, forest. Rather, *woodland* was country in which the fields were small and were surrounded by ditches and walls made of the earth thrown up in digging the ditches. And often hedges or trees were grown in these walls, to give this kind of countryside the look of being wooded, in contrast to the open fields of the champion land.

. . . .

The boundaries of landscape are international, and the same contrasts were recognized on the southern shore of the English Channel as were recognized on the northern. Nowhere were the two kinds of landscape set apart by a sharp line like a surveyed frontier, but in a long-range view the provinces of each are plain. The country of the big villages—what is called the open-field country—stretched in a long band across England from the North Sea coast to the Channel. Crossing the Channel, it reappeared in northeastern France and went on across the Rhine into the lands of old held or conquered by the Germans, and into Denmark and Sweden. In the peninsulas and islands of the Western Ocean ruled the land of small walled fields and scattered settlement, in Brittany and western Normandy in France, in Cornwall and Devon in England, in Wales and the northwestern English shires bordering on Wales, in Ireland, and, at least so far as scattered settlements are concerned, in Scotland. Finally, to the east as well as to the west of the open fields, in the southeastern corner of England, especially Kent, and in Flanders, is a country of old enclosures and scattered settlement.

. . . .

II

The influences which determine the character of landscapes are of three kinds: geographical, technical, and social. The geographical factors include the terrain, the soils, and the climate. The technical factors include the ways in which the people who live on the land in question make a living from it: what tame animals they keep and how they care for them, what grains they know, what implements they use and how they use them, and so forth. These first two kinds of factors are economic factors. The third kind of factors, the social factors, include the customs according to which particular groups of people work together in making a living and in carrying on the other businesses of a society. Something must be said about each of these in talking about the difference between champion and woodland country. But no one of the three kinds of factors is independent of the other two. For instance, grain cannot be grown in a swamp.

The sort of thing geographers have to say about the way men settle on the land can be illustrated in the matter of soils. In France, they point out, the land of scattered settlements, both in Flanders and in the west, is by and large the land of the soils which hold the water. The big villages, on the other hand, lie on the soils which allow rain to soak through them quickly. For, in the first kind of country, surface water is abundant and habitation can be dispersed, whereas in the other kind of country springs are rare and wells must be sunk deep; accordingly, people come together in numbers by the sources of drink for their cattle and themselves.

Unhappily, the coincidence of soils with kinds of human settlement is only a rough one. The weakness of arguments which trace the differences between woodland and champion landscape to one or another geographical influence is that woodland is often found where champion country should by rights have been, champion country where woodland should have been. People of the present day have become attached to the economic interpretation of history. And they have become used to hearing about manufacturers in fact changing their methods in order to obtain greater efficiency. Accordingly, they always overrate the importance of economic motives in the behavior of men. Of these supposed motives, the desire of men to make the most of their geographical environment is one. To be sure, the economic motives underlie all others, for most men have always been determined to get enough to eat and to keep themselves warm. But once they have worked out techniques which satisfy these needs reasonably well, they are slow to make them more efficient. They do not adopt such of the methods other people use as are better than their own, because they do not hear of them. And they do not conceive of the possibility of themselves reflecting upon their methods so as to invent better ones or to adapt the old ones more accurately to the requirements of the economic environment. They neither adopt nor adapt. This is especially true of times when useful information spread slowly and the feeling that it was wrong to change established custom was stronger than it is now. In those days a farmer would do his work in the same way as his neighbors did it and as his father taught him, and would not dream that another was possible. And when he moved into a new country he would try to adapt the country to his customs rather than his customs to the country.

A proof of this is at hand. The old world contrast between villages and scattered settlement repeated itself in the new world. The first colonists in Massachusetts settled in big villages and tried to establish open common fields like those they had known in the east of England. In time the "commons" had to be abandoned, save in the form of parks, but the big village remained and became the New England town. But the first Frenchmen in Quebec came from woodland country in Brittany and Normandy, and settled, as at home, not in villages but in scattered farms. Villages grew up later, but only when churches were built and the houses of shopkeepers and tradesmen clustered around these general meeting places. The colonists, then, made little attempt to adapt themselves, at least in the beginning, to specifically American conditions. They lived as they were used to living in the old country.

What was true of the French and English in America was perhaps true of their distant forefathers who made the woodland and champion landscapes of Europe: that they were moved less by the geographical features of the countries in which they settled than by the customs which had been handed down to them from previous generations.

. . . .

The most interesting features of the woodland countryside were the small groups of people by which it was inhabited. The settlements were dispersed, but they were not isolated farms, each the home of a man with his wife, children, and hired men, like those of most of the rural parts of the United States. Not, at least, in early times. To be sure, isolated farms existed in land which was being cleared of forest, but in the land of old arable this was not so. The woodland settlements were somewhere between a farm and a big village in size. They seem seldom to have been made up of more than twenty families, and there are signs that a hamlet of this sort was the natural group of homesteads of people using in common a single plow and having their cattle in a single herd.[1]

Whatever the economic bond, the social bond that held the dwellers in the woodland hamlets together may in the old days have been kinship, kinship in the extended family of descendants of a near and common ancestor. Certainly in out-of-way parts of Ireland today the sentiments and ceremonies associated with the kin are more elaborate than they ever were in the country of the open-field villages. But the villagers made up for their falling short in feelings of kinship by their neighborliness in the larger community. And after centuries of living in hamlets or villages, many of the attitudes characteristic of each, impressed by the older generations on their children, must still be vigorous even in peoples who have abandoned their old homes.

It is a mistake, then, to look on landscapes as the result of isolated activities of men, economic or social; for such activities are in fact seldom isolated but are found in a state of mutual dependence with many other activities. What is more, these activities are mutually dependent not only directly but also indirectly, in that they all take part in the functioning of the organic wholes or systems which are called societies, and these wholes are greater than and unlike the sums of their parts. Landscapes must be conceived of as the physical shell of such organic social wholes, each perpetuating through the centuries its particular organization.

III

The techniques people use in making a living are one of the influences determining what sort of landscape they form, just as living techniques are one of the influences determining many of the features

[1] See F. Seebohm, *Tribal Custom in Anglo-Saxon Law,* p. 36, quoting *Ancient Laws of Wales,* ii, 693.

of a society. Before the villages of the Middle Ages are described it is well to talk about some of these methods. We of the present day are inclined to think of ourselves as the first people who have used elaborate techniques. But the older traditional techniques were in some ways as elaborate as our own, if not as mechanical, and they required a vast amount of skill and experience. Practically speaking, a man cannot become a farmer unless he is brought up as one. The necessary training takes years to acquire. If this is true today, when farmers can buy most of the articles they need, how much more is it true of a time not so long ago when farmers had to clothe themselves and make their own tools as well as raise their own food? A village of the Middle Ages usually supported a smith, who made the plow-irons and the horseshoes, but nearly everything else a villager had to do for himself. He had to be master of a number of rather elaborate skills.

. . . .

Most of these techniques were handed down from fathers to sons, from mothers to daughters, substantially unchanged. Indeed, each little district was likely to develop its own varieties of the standard tools or cloths and maintain their individuality from generation to generation. When any of these goods were especially well made, demand for them grew among outsiders, and the district in which the skill was developed might become a center of manufacturing and trade. Our own age is clearly not the only one which has made inventions, and from the discovery of the use of fire, in the dark ages, on, clever men have worked out new devices, and these by force of their usefulness have been imitated over immense distances and have made older methods obsolete. Such once must have been the flail and the winnowing-fan, and though we now look on them as crude implements, we should be lucky to remember how to make them if by any chance we should lose our modern threshing machines. For they save time, like any modern piece of machinery, and in their day their invention must have seemed just as marvellous. But there is another thing to remember about inventions. That is that they do not often and can seldom come singly. There is little point in learning how to cultivate cereals if at the same time you do not know a way of separating the grain from the straw and the wheat from the chaff.

One particular invention had much to do with the form of the open-fields of the champion villages. That was the plow, the most important implement of agriculture. And it was a true invention, for the plow, with its heavy frame, iron share and coulter, and mould-board, seems to have displaced the crooked stick drawn through the sod with a pair of oxen which is and was used by many primitive peoples, European and other. This displacement in some countries was still going on in recent times. The advantages of the plow are that it breaks up the ground to a greater depth than the crooked stick, and with its mould-board, always on the right-hand side, turns over the furrow. This second feature allows the plow to become an instrument for drainage. For in the Middle Ages it was the custom to plow land in narrow strips. The plow would begin at the outside of the strip and go round and round the strip, from the outside in, always turning the earth toward the middle of the strip. After a few plowings of this sort, the earth would be taken from the two outer edges of the strip and heaped up in the middle in a ridge, and in wet weather the ridges would stay dry, while the water collected in the troughs between the ridges. Where people chiefly lived in England in ancient times and most likely through the Roman occupation was on the high downs. Perhaps the conquest of the valleys was possible only after the introduction of the heavy plow with the mould-board, accompanied by the technique of ridge-plowing, had enabled people to drain the low-lying arable land.[2]

IV

In the *campagne* of northwestern Europe in the Middle Ages, the village was the farming unit. The village was a unit in that its houses, each set in a close,[3] were all near together, in rows on either side of a long street or more planlessly clustered around the parish church. The village was a unit in that the fields which spread out in a ring around the houses and closes were village fields, cultivated according to a rotation of crops which was customary and binding on every villager. The commonest practice was to divide the village fields into three great sectors—the fields, properly so-called. Each year one of these sectors would lie fallow; one would be seeded to winter grain (wheat or rye), and one to spring grain, where, as the folk-song says,

Oats, peas, beans, and barley grows.

In the next year, the fallow field would become the winter wheat field,

[2] See A. Birnie, "Ridge Cultivation in Scotland," *The Scottish Historical Review*, xxiv, 194 ff. There are ways of plowing ridges other than the one described.

[3] The custom of the Germans in having a certain amount of land around their houses struck Tacitus by its contrast with the custom of the Italians in building their houses against each other, wall to wall (*Germania*, 16).

the winter wheat field, the spring wheat field, and so on in succession through the centuries. The village was also a unit in that the cattle of the village, under the tending of village herdsmen, ranged in one herd over the stubble of the fallow field and other village pastures. Finally, the woods and wastes within its borders were kept for the common use of the villagers. That the village was a unit means simply that the sentiments of people, according to which they worked together as a village in raising their food, dominated those according to which they might have worked as separate families. Unquestionably this was true in early times, but the physical framework and arrangements of the village remained long after the sentiments which had determined them had disappeared.

The village, then, was what it was because the villagers worked together, and if a man works face to face with his neighbors day after day, year after year, perhaps the feeling is encouraged that he should share equally with them in the fruit of their common labor. But whatever the reason for it, the arrangement of the big villages was such that every villager shared with his neighbors in the wealth of the village, which was mostly land. His stake in the village consisted of a house and close in the village proper, a share in the use of the village woods, wastes, and pastures, and a number of acres in the village fields, so divided that an equal amount lay in each field. By this means the villager was assured of a steady supply of grain year by year, no matter which field lay fallow. Moreover, in no field did the holding of a villager lie as a compact block of land, but as a series of narrow strips, consisting of a number of the parallel and adjacent ridges made in plowing, scattered all over the village fields, and divided from the strips of his neighbors by lines of turf left unplowed, or simply by the furrows between ridges. By this means, the villager was assured that he shared proportionately with his fellows in the bad and good soils, in the favorable and unfavorable locations in the village fields. But also, since his lands lay scattered in small strips, and the fields were submitted to an unvarying rotation of crops and fallow pasture, the villager was forced to cultivate the same grains as his fellow-villagers and at the same times. All these provisions put out of the question a villager's setting up permanent walls or hedges around his land or building his house in the fields outside the village proper. This is why the country of the mediaeval villages is open-field country.

The holdings of the villagers were not only scattered in the same proportions over the bad and good lands of the village, they were also in fact, for any given class of villagers, equal in size. But as far back as the records go, the mediaeval village was never a classless society. Two main classes of villagers were well enough set apart to be called by special names, and the equality of holdings held good only within these classes or their subdivisions. Even more clearly than most class structures, that of the village was related to the division of labor. Oxen were the most important single requirement in tillage, for many of them were needed to drag the crude and heavy plow through the ground— eight made the commonest plow team of the Middle Ages—and the class that a man belonged to depended on whether he owned and used plow-oxen or worked with his hands. The upper class were the villagers proper, who possessed plow-oxen, yoked them with those of their fellows in plowing, and held a substantial number of acres in the village fields. The lower class were the so-called cotters, who possessed no plow-oxen and, as their name implies, a cottage and a close, but only a few acres, if any, in the fields. The cotters furnished the villagers properly so-called with the necessary supply of spare hands.

Last of all, however standardized, traditional, and unvarying this open-field village plan may seem to be, it could not work unless it could be adjusted to conditions which vary from year to year. Farmers, for one thing, have never been able to take the weather for granted. Villagers cooperated in plowing; therefore they had to agree among themselves every season as to when plowing should begin. They had to choose herdsmen, make regulations about pasturage, meadows, harvest-laborers. Not least, the open-field system left many chances for clashes between villagers. Such matters seemed to have been settled in village meetings, held separately or together with the court of the feudal lord. Not in England only, but all over Europe, there has always been a large measure of local self-government.

V

No one feature of a society can for long be usefully considered apart from the other features of the society. This is as much true of the society of the Middle Ages as it is of any other. Outside the Church, the two most important institutions of that society were the towns and the feudal-manorial system, and there is something to be said about the relation of the village to each of these. Towns were set apart from the country in the Middle Ages in more ways than by walls. Foreign and long-distance trade centered in the towns, and they were mostly free of feudal and manorial arrangements. More important, perhaps, towns were the chief means by which able people from the lower rose into the upper classes, and this is probably something that must go on in any society if it is to be kept healthy. But even now, and much more so in old times, a man has to get out of the community he was brought up in if he is to rise in the world. The towns took care of this. Ambitious plowboys moved to the towns to escape the bonds of village life. And if they prospered, their daughters might marry into the landed gentry.

Though town and village were separate worlds, they were worlds which were similarly organized. Many of the towns began as farming villages, and some of them, especially the smaller ones, always kept their common fields. The countrymen who deserted their villages to contribute to the great growth of boroughs which began in the tenth century clearly did not wholly get rid of the habits their mothers and fathers had taught them. People today talk much about town-planning and succeed in doing very little about it. But the open-field villages were arranged according to a plan which was standard and customary over much of Europe, and the people who made the towns of the Middle Ages imitated it as far as the difference in occupations allowed. At least in the early stages of borough history, the tenements of the burgesses were equal, like those of open-field villagers, and every burgess was supposed to share equally with every other burgess in whatever bargain any one of them made. The townsfolk, too, governed themselves, by means of an elected council. These arrangements, similar in town and country, are important means of reckoning what were the fundamental sentiments of the common people of the Middle Ages.

The ruling and warring classes of the Middle Ages were supported by tillers of the soil who paid them labor, food, and money rents. There has been much controversy as to whether or not the villages of Europe were originally independent communities upon whom lords later thrust themselves. Talk about origins which are not recorded and cannot be observed is usually inexpedient, but there is this to be said. The so-called manorial system, with its great estates and its labor services, was in full force only in the parts of Europe where the large villages and open-field system existed, and it is possible that the heavy services of plowing and other agricultural labor which the villagers of the Middle Ages, in coöperation, were bound to render towards the cultivation of the demesne of the lord of the manor could have been exacted only where the villagers were in the habit of working together in the same way in cultivating their own lands. Perhaps it is significant that in later times a job of plowing or other work which villagers as a body did to help out a needy neighbor was called a boon-day, and a boon-day was once the name given to such work when rendered to the lord.[4] The men of Kent and Flanders were freemen by 1300, that is, were bound to do few labor services for their lords or none at all, although there were many unfree in the lands around them, and the reason for it may have been that neither the open-field system nor its concomitant, the typical manor, existed in these two countries.

. . . .

VI

The first thing to be said in general about the open-field village system was that, in economic terms, it worked. Ridge-plowing is a way of draining land; a bare fallow is a way of restoring land exhausted by crops. Even if better ways of doing these things have since been invented, it must not be forgotten that the old ways did do the job. However much people suffered from famine and other hardships, open-field agriculture supported an increasing population for at least a thousand years. The system even gave some classes a security which they lost when the system was abandoned. A poor man in England in the old days was sure of a few acres of croft and could send a cow to graze on the commons of the village. Afterwards, such a man was wholly dependent on his wages as a farm laborer.

The open-field system worked in that it kept a large number of people alive. But even when the crudities of the farming techniques are left out of account, it is clear that the system was not efficient. For its arrangements were dictated by custom as well as by the economic situation. A plowman plowed in a day, not as much land as he could, but as much as was recognized by custom as a fair day's job of plowing. He plowed with eight oxen, not because eight oxen were just enough to draw his plow through the soil, for the soils varied in heaviness, but because it was the custom to plow with eight oxen. And it is likely that he began to plow, not on the days each year when the weather was the very best for beginning to plow, but on the days each year when it was customary to begin to plow, and these were tied to the religious calendar.

When the first scientific farmers, like Arthur Young, ran up against

[4] E. Gutch, *Folklore of the North Riding of Yorkshire* (*York and the Ainsty*), p. 338; M. C. Balfour and N. W. Thomas, *Folklore of Northumberland*, p. 122.

this sort of behavior at the end of the eighteenth century, they of course cursed it as folly. It was folly to plow with eight oxen, when two horses could do the work. It was folly to cleave to the old three-field rotation when turnips and the grasses could be introduced. The ways of the scientific farmers won out, but they forgot, just as those who today talk about "America's capacity to produce" forget, that capacity to produce depends on two factors, not one. It depends on techniques and implements of production. It depends also on the feelings of the men who carry out these techniques. The theorists talk as if the second factor could be taken for granted. It cannot.

The open-field system seems a strangely formalized one to people of the present day, especially if they are intellectuals and are not used to working for their living from dawn to dusk in close contact with their fellow-men. They do not appreciate that in any such situation a set of customs are built up which prescribe what the conduct of every member of the group which is working together shall be toward every other member of the group. These customs tend to fall into a fixed and definite pattern. Behind them is the force of sentiment, not the logic of the economic situation. Indeed, they often run counter to the demands of the economic situation, and in many modern factories make their presence manifest in restriction of output by the workers. Conforming to this set of customs, a member of the group is able, without taking conscious thought, to work with the other members of the group as fellow human beings. Successful cooperation is impossible without such a set of customs.

· ·

Such arrangements as the day's work of plowing, the eight-ox team, the scattering of village holdings in small strips, and the compulsory rotation of crops, clearly did not run utterly counter to the demands of the economic situation, and could not, if the village was to survive. At the same time, they were not perfectly adapted to the economic situation. There is a gap, because two considerations, not one, determine the dispositions made by any group of people working together to make their living: the techniques they use, and the customs according to which they cooperate in using these techniques in a manner satisfactory to them as human beings. These customs are the important thing about any society and they are the important thing about mediaeval villages, for the villages were simply the units of land and of people within which they were in force.

· ·

SUGGESTIONS FOR ADDITIONAL READING

Marc Bloch, "Le Problème des régimes agraires," *Mélanges historiques,* Vol. II (Paris, 1963).

J. P. Chambers, *Laxton: The Last English Open Field Village,* London, 1964.

H. L. Gray, *English Field Systems,* Cambridge, Mass., 1915. New edition 1959.

George C. Homans, *English Villagers of the Thirteenth Century,* Cambridge, Mass., 1941.

C. S. Orwin, "Observations on the Open Fields," *The Economic History Review,* Vol. VIII, No. 2 (1938).

THE RISE OF INTENSIVE HUSBANDRY IN THE LOW COUNTRIES *

B. H. Slicher van Bath

Some of the most important early advances in agriculture during the modern era were made in the Low Countries. It is not without reason that this region has been called "the school-room of the Agricultural Revolution." The selection that follows shows the progress of agriculture there and its relation to geographic, demographic, and economic factors. B. H. Slicher van Bath, one of Europe's most distinguished agricultural historians, is director of the Department of Agricultural History at the Landbouwhogeschool at Wageningen, Holland.

During the seventeenth, eighteenth, and the beginning of the nineteenth centuries the Low Countries—including modern Belgium, French Flanders and the Netherlands—had great fame in agriculture. Visitors from abroad—from Great Britain, France, Germany, Italy, Sweden, and even from the United States—made tours through these

---

* From J. S. Bromley and E. H. Kossman, eds., *Britain and the Netherlands* (London: Chatto and Windus, 1960), pp. 130–53. Reprinted by permission of the editors and Chatto and Windus Ltd.

provinces. They studied the state of Dutch agriculture and the methods used there. Having returned to their country, they propagated the new things they had learned. One would think the Low Countries were in this period a farmer's paradise, or better still a paradise for visiting gentlemen-farmers, who felt themselves individually far ahead of their own agriculturally underdeveloped countries. Their monotonous, sometimes pig-headed, advice to their countrymen to follow Dutch methods testifies more often to their knowledge of book-farming than to their having an open mind on the real needs of their own countries. There the circumstances were mostly so utterly different from those of the densely populated and economically highly developed Netherlands that it was not possible to imitate Dutch agricultural methods without considerable modification. For this reason, the results of the immigration of Dutch farmers or of the importation of Dutch cattle did not as a rule fulfil the high expectations held of them. Even in this century, textbooks for the instruction of Italian schoolboys have contained a circumstantial description of Flemish agriculture, perhaps interesting to them, but not really very useful.

From this example one can guess the great influence which radiated from the Low Countries. Nor is it difficult to understand that this influence was strongly felt in Great Britain, the neighbour land across the North Sea. A modern English authority has declared that "our farming and gardening debt to that country [viz. Holland] is very great." [1] But the history of Dutch influence on British agriculture has yet to be written. Until then, our knowledge remains fragmentary, connected with such names as those of Sir Richard Weston, Lord Townshend, Bakewell, Sir John Sinclair, Thomas Radcliff, the Earl of Stair, Andrew Fletcher of Saltoun, James Meikle, Bartholomew Rocque, Patrick Neill, and William Speechley.[2] They propagated new rotation

[1] G. E. Fussell, *More Old English Farming Books* (1950), p. 146. Mr. Fussell is preparing a book on the subject. The passages on Dutch agriculture in J. E. Thorold Rogers, *Six Centuries of Work and Wages*, II (1884), pp. 452–4, are flattering enough, but not as exact as we should like: Gabriel Plattes (p. 455) was not a Dutchman by descent, no more was Samuel Hartlib (p. 459) a Dutchman by birth. The same in J. Kulischer, *Allgemeine Wirtschaftsgeschichte, Die Neuzeit*, II (1929), p. 39. However, see G. E. Fussell, *The Old English Farming Books from Fitzherbert to Tull, 1523 to 1730* (1947), p. 41.

[2] [Sir Richard Weston], *A Discourse of Husbandrie used in Brabant and Flanders* (2nd edn. 1652). Sir John Sinclair, *Hints regarding the agricultural state of the Netherlands compared with that of Great Britain* (1815). Thomas Radcliff, *A report on the agriculture of Eastern and Western Flanders* (1819). Pat. Neill, *Journal of a horticultural tour through some parts of Flanders, Holland and the North of France, in the autumn of 1817* (1823).

40569   College of St. Francis
LIBRARY

systems on the fields; the cultivation of such fodder crops as clover, lucerne, burnet, timothy grass, and the famous turnips; new types of ploughs, of a light construction like those used in Gelderland, and ploughs with a Dutch wheel coulter; and the winnowing machine, which was probably introduced into Europe from China by the Dutch.[3]

The cultivation of hops on a large scale for the preparation of beer, as of cole-seed and buckwheat, originated in the Low Countries. Of course, we should not exaggerate the significance of Dutch agriculture, but I believe one is not claiming too much for it in saying that during the seventeenth and eighteenth centuries Dutch farmers excelled in stockbreeding and dairy produce, in the cultivation of commercial crops, in horticulture, and in the invention and use of simple and cheap tools.

A general view of the technical improvements in Dutch agriculture has been published in the Reports of the International Historical Congress at Rome in 1955, so it is not necessary to repeat that here.[4] Briefly, the improvements amounted to the disappearance of the fallow; the related cultivation of fodder crops; and bed- and row-cultivation. High yields were obtained by heavy fertilizing and by applying much labour to a small area.

Already in the Middle Ages the three-yearly crop-rotation of winter corn, summer corn, and fallow was not practised everywhere. In this system the fallow was necessary owing to the shortage of manure and the rapid growth of weeds which goes with corn-growing. Corn will soon find itself overgrown by weeds. After every two years it is necessary to plough the land several times in order to clear it of weeds.

There were three ways to improve the three-yearly crop-rotation system and so diminish the area which could not be used for cultivation:

1. An intensified system of cultivation with fallow not in the third, but in the fourth, fifth, or sixth year. On the original fallow, pulse and corn were cultivated. The oldest record of the cultivation of beans

---

Lord Townshend (Turnip Townshend) had been ambassador in the Netherlands. The black horse of Bakewell had Frisian blood. The Earl of Stair imported a plough from Holland in 1730 (G. E. Fussell, *The Farmer's Tools*, 1500–1900 (1952), pp. 45–6). Andrew Fletcher of Saltoun sent James Meikle to Holland for imitating a Dutch mill for making pot barley. He imported into England the winnowing mill (Fussell, *ibid.*, p. 158). Rocque and Speechley were horticulturists (G. E. Fussell, *More Old English Farming Books*, pp. 44–5, 146).

[3] Fussell, *The Farmer's Tools*, pp. 37, 44–5, 158.

[4] B. H. Slicher van Bath, "Agriculture in the Low Countries," in *Relazioni del X congresso internazionale di scienze storiche*, IV (1955), pp. 169–203.

and corn on the fallow dates back to 1328 and concerns the coastal regions of French Flanders, north west of Cassel.[5]

2. A system of convertible husbandry of arable land and pasture: that is, winter corn (one year), summer corn (one year), fallow (one year), and pasture (three or six years). Because a larger area was thus used for grassland, more cattle could be kept. This meant in turn a far larger production of manure for the arable land. This system is probably first mentioned in 1323, in a region just south of the city walls of Ghent, certainly in 1368 at St Pieters ter Aalst (Ghent), and in 1372 at Lede near Alost.[6]

3. A system with cultivation of fodder crops. Here we may discern:

(a) The cultivation of fodder crops on the fallow during the original fallow-year. First mentioned in the second half of the fifteenth century: 1480 at Nieuwerkerken near St Trond, cultivation of vetches; 1491 at Stayen, near the same town, cultivation of summer crops not precisely indicated; 1498 near Louvain, fodder crops for pasturing.

(b) The cultivation of fodder crops, such as turnips or spurry as an after-crop, sown after the corn was harvested. We have records of this method from the beginning and middle of the fifteenth century; 1404 at Messelbroek near Aarschot, the cultivation of turnips; 1446 at Rooigem near Ghent, leaves of turnips for pasturing; 1447 at Geel, again the cultivation of turnips.[7]

---

[5] H. Pirenne, Le soulèvement de la Flandre maritime de 1323–1328 (1900), pp. vi–vii (introduction), 208: plaint of Jehan de Saint-Nicholay, Bourbourgh, who had to leave the country during the troubles and whose house and barns were burnt and who could not cultivate his arable. "Item encore perdi lidis Jehans, pour la cause dessusdite, les esplois de 24 mesures de terre dont il avoit 8 mesures de blé, 8 mesures d'avaine et 8 mesures que fèves que trémois, dont cascune mesure l'une parmi l'autre valut 40 s. par.; motent 48 lib. Item perdi lidis Jehans 2 mesures de herbage qui valut à 20 s. le mesure; valent 40 s." The mesure is somewhat larger than an acre (0·44 HA.); trémois is corn of three months which is cut in spring and used as fodder. ["Likewise also lost by the said Jehan, for the aforementioned cause, the profit from 24 mesures of land, whence he had 8 mesures in wheat, 8 mesures in oats, and 8 mesures in beans or in trémois of which (the profit from) each mesure, one like the other, valued 40 shillings; total 48 pounds. Likewise lost by the said Jehan (the profit from) 2 mesures of meadow-land which valued at 20s the mesure and were worth 40s." Editor's note.]

[6] P. Lindemans, Geschiedenis van de Landbouw in België (2 vols., 1952), I, pp. 83–4, notes 32 and 36.

[7] P. Lindemans, ibid., I, pp. 412 (note 45), 439; A. Verhulst, "Bijdragen tot de studie van de agrarische struktuur in het Vlaamse land: 2. Het probleem van

Of the fodder crops, the cultivation of vetches is for the first time recorded in 1278 at Tournay;[8] of turnips, in 1404 at Messelbroek near Aarschot; of spurry, in 1426 at Maaseik (Belgian Limburg); of broom, in 1490 at Nieuwerkerken near St Trond.[9]

The rotation system described by Sir Richard Weston, as he saw it in use in the Waes region between Ghent and Antwerp in 1644, was the base of the famous Norfolk system, which achieved such success at the end of the seventeenth and in the eighteenth centuries.[10] In 1800 a similar system was still in use in Brabant, as can be observed on a farm at Edegem south of Antwerp.[11]

.   .   .   .

In 1669, in some parts of England, turnips were already sown in the field and they were used as food for cattle and swine.[12] In 1686 they were introduced, together with flax, on the Godinton Estate in Kent.[13]

A special Flemish custom was bed-cultivation in long, narrow, curved fields in which good drainage was achieved. By shifting the beds in the field a little each year, the farmers also managed to use all the soil of the field in the course of some years. With this system of cultivation in beds, probably taken over from horticulture, row-cultivation can easily be applied. These beds are represented in the miniatures of the *Breviarium Grimani* and other calendars of the sixtenth century.[14]

It is not known when row-cultivation was used in corn-growing. But it is very common in the culture of some fodder crops and of commercial crops, such as cole-seed, hops, madder, and tobacco. Among these, the culture of tobacco has left no record earlier than 1623, near

de verdwijning van de braak in de Vlaamse landbouw (XIIIe-XVIIe eeuw)," in *Natuurwetenschappelijk tijdschrift*, 38 (1956), pp. 213–19.

[8] Vetches in 1360 at St Lievens-Houtem, west of Alost; in 1394–95 at Middelaar, south of Nymegen.

[9] P. Lindemans, *op. cit.*, I, pp. 427, 436, 439, 446 (note 7).

[10] W. G. Hoskins, "English Agriculture in the 17th and 18th Centuries," in *Relazioni del X congresso internazionale di scienze storiche*, IV (1955), p. 215.

[11] J. N. Schwerz, *Anleitung zur Kenntniss der belgischen Landwirthschaft*, II (1808), pp. 387–405; a new crop are the potatoes.

[12] John Worlidge, *Systema agriculturae* (1669), pp. 42–3. E. Kerridge, "Turnip husbandry in High Suffolk," in *The Economic History Review*, sec. ser., vol. VIII (1956), pp. 390–2.

[13] E. C. Lodge, *The Account Book of a Kentish Estate, 1616–1704* (1907), p. xxx.

[14] P. Lindemans, *op. cit.*, I, p. 155, note 1. The author does not mention any written records.

Amersfoort.[15] Cole-seed, madder, and hops, however, are all mentioned in the fourteenth century: cole-seed in 1358, imported from Amsterdam into Antwerp,[16] madder in 1325 in Zeeland.[17] The brewing of beer with hops came into use in the first quarter of the same century.[18] At the end of the fifteenth century there was a centre of hop-cultivation in the south of Holland and in North Brabant (Gouda c. 1361; Breda c. 1373; southern parts of Holland in 1494 and 1514).[19] Row-cultivation for some commercial crops must, therefore, have been in use since the fourteenth century.

Row-cultivation in corn-growing was still unknown in 1803 in Flanders, when Diercxsen made some experiments there.[20] Lindemans is of opinion, however, that in a very primitive manner—by sowing in the furrow—row-cultivation for this purpose was practised as early as the second half of the sixteenth century.[21] We know that in the province of Groningen in the eighteenth century certain tools for row-cultivation were used: a marking-tool to make the furrows, a seeding-horn and horse-drawn seeding-barrels for sowing corn, buckwheat, cole-seed, pulse, etc.[22] Here the row-cultivation was probably introduced by Palatine Mennonites at the beginning of the eighteenth century.

The culture of commercial crops requires extreme care. Deep digging, heavy fertilizing, and repeated weeding are necessary. The required fertilizers could be got from the stock-raising areas and from the towns (which supplied ashes from wood and peat, compost, and privy-manure). Deep digging (often with the spade) and repeated

[15] V. R. Y. Croesen, "Tabakscultuur in Nederland," in *Agronomisch-Historisch Jaarboek*, I (1940), p. 4.

[16] F. H. Mertens and K. L. Torfs, *Geschiedenis van Antwerpen*, II (1846), p. 280.

[17] C. Wiskerke, "De geschiedenis van het meekrapbedrijf in Nederland," in *Economisch-Historisch Jaarboek*, XV (1952), pp. 14–16.

[18] G. Doorman, *De middeleeuwse brouwerij en de gruit* (1955), pp. 40–1; J. van Loenen, *De Haarlemse brouwindustrie vóór 1600* (1950), p. 31.

[19] W. J. Sangers, *Gegevens betreffende de ontwikkeling van de Nederlandse tuinbouw* (1953), pp. 7, 12; *Enqueste ende informatie . . . van den schiltaelen . . . van Hollant ende Vrieslant . . . 1494* (ed. R. Fruin, 1876); *Informacie up den statet . . . van de steden ende dorpen van Hollant ende Vrieslant . . . 1514* (1860).

[20] J. N. Schwerz, *op. cit.*, I (1807), pp. 259, 279–83; J. M. G. van der Poel, *Heren en boeren*, Agronomisch-Historische Bijdragen, II (1949), p. 7.

[21] P. Lindemans, *op. cit.*, II, p. 53, on the ground of an engraving of this period.

[22] Sc. Trip, "Manier van zaaijen meest in de Veen-Kolonien in het Departement Groningen in gebruik; en verdere bewerking van het gezaaide, met eene afbeelding van den goten- of vorenjager, en zoogenoemden blikken zaaihoorn," in *Magazijn van vaderlandschen landbouw*, V (1810), pp. 222–31.

weeding meant much labour. This is an intensive form of husbandry, therefore, in which small-holdings predominated and which enabled a large number of people to make a decent living on a small area of land. When flax was cultivated, a mere acre and a half sufficed to sustain a family.[23]

The application of much labour to small areas is only possible in regions which combine dense population with agricultural produce of high value. Here, on the one hand, the supply of labour could be plentiful, the cost of labour in relation to the total output tolerably low. On the other hand, the towns with their many industries required the commercial crops, while a large linen industry flourished in the villages.

Nevertheless, this dense population wanted food, above all, cereals. But only at the expense of corn-growing could the cultivation of commercial crops develop, so corn had to be imported from elsewhere— mainly, in practice, from the Baltic. Specialization indeed, in the form of cattle-breeding, cultivation of commercial crops and horticulture, required the import of corn in large quantities. Only then could the complicated interlocking system of agriculture and industry function to the fullest advantage.

In these preliminary remarks I have tried to sketch the main features of the development of intensive husbandry in the Low Countries. Not all the phenomena can be dated, but many of them were first mentioned in the thirteenth, fourteenth, or fifteenth centuries. Of course, this does not mean that everywhere in the Low Countries during that period the fallow had disappeared, or that row-cultivation and cultivation of fodder crops were universally applied. It was a slow process, and even as such it took place only in some of the western provinces: Flanders, the western part of Brabant, Zeeland, Holland, and Friesland. About the progress of intensive agriculture we know relatively little. Moreover, there are also gaps in our knowledge of the density and mutations in the size of the population during the Middle Ages.

Many geographical, technical and economic questions are still unanswered. I shall discuss some of them.

I

The *geographical* problem has nothing to do with narrow-minded feelings of national pride, but it is still unclear what was the geographical distribution of the new methods, the new crops, and the

[23] So J. H. von Thünen, *Der isolierte Staat in Beziehung auf Landwirthschaft und Nationalökonomie,* I (2nd impr., 1842), p. 311.

new tools in the northern and southern parts of the Low Countries. The two volumes of Lindemans' highly important *Agricultural History of Belgium* [24] give us a good view of the development of agriculture in Flanders and Brabant. An adequate work on the agricultural history of the Northern Netherlands is still lacking. So our knowledge is geographically very one-sided.

Formulating my suppositions very carefully, I think it probable that the cultivation of cole-seed, buckwheat, hops, and perhaps clover originated in the north, and that it was from there that it spread throughout Europe.

In the sixteenth century rape-seed, which had previously been the usual crop, was displaced by cole-seed. This is a very profitable plant, because the oil cakes (which remain after the oil has been crushed out) can be given to the cattle for winter fodder. In Zeeland this was already done in 1557.[25] In the southern provinces cole-seed is first mentioned—according to Lindemans—at Bogaarden, southwest of Brussels, in 1562 and then in 1568.[26] The first records of cole-seed in the north are already two centuries earlier—in 1358, 1359, and 1366. There it is mentioned together with rape-seed, so a mistake is not probable. When the Count of Flanders founded a staple of ·merchandise in the city of Antwerp on behalf of the merchants of Amsterdam and Holland—and a year later for the merchants of Utrecht—the merchandise is specified as fat wares, butter, cheese, grease, lard, hides, eggs, rape-seed, cole-seed, mustard-seed, hemp-seed honey, and virgin-honey.[27] These are all products indigenous in Holland and Utrecht. In Friesland cole-seed was perhaps cultivated as early as the sixteenth century.[28]

In the sixteenth and seventeenth centuries the culture of cole-seed spread to Artois, the German Rhineland, Schleswig Holstein, etc. In England cole-seed was imported by such Dutch colonists as the well-known Sir Cornelius Vermuyden, and by Walloons and Picards. Originally it was only cultivated there in the eastern coastal counties. The

[24] P. Lindemans, *Geschiedenis van de landbouw in België*, 2 vols., 1952.

[25] M. J. Boerendonk, *Historische studie over den Zeeuwschen landbouw* (1935), p. 260.

[26] P. Lindemans, *op. cit.*, II, p. 279, note 22; earlier perhaps in 1515 (*ibid.*, note 24). Cole-seed is recorded in the fifteenth century at Bousbecques on the Belgian frontier near Menin: J. H. Clapham and E. Power, *The Cambridge Economic History of Europe*, I (1942), p. 154.

[27] F. H. Mertens and K. L. Torfs, *Geschiedenis van Antwerpen*, II (1846), pp. 280, 553. F. Prims, *Geschiedenis van Antwerpen*, V, 3 (1935), pp. 21 (22 Apl. 1358), 27 (15 Nov. 1359), 51 (3 Sept. 1366).

[28] J. J. Spahr van der Hoek and O. Postma, *Geschiedenis van de Friese landbouw*, I (1952), pp. 122, 124, 125.

English farmers had to ask Dutch advice about the best way of cultivation and the use of the pods and oilcakes for winter fodder. New seed
had to be imported from the Low Countries when the English seed
deteriorated. An imitation of the Dutch method of threshing the cole-
seed on a threshing-cloth (on account of the loss of the seed) is recorded
in Lincolnshire.

Not fully in accordance with the importation of the cultivation of
cole-seed by the Dutch into England is the exportation of cole-seed as
early as 1602, and later in 1639 and 1640, from Boston to Rotterdam,
Amsterdam, and Middelburg.[29] From the same port rape-seed, oilcakes
of rape-seed, line-seed, mustard-seed, and hemp-seed were exported to
Holland and Zeeland. On the other hand, flax, hops, and madder were
imported from Holland into England.

Buckwheat makes its first appearance in historical sources in an account dated 1394-95 as payment in kind to the duke of Gelderland by
a farmer at Middelaar, south of Nymegen.[30] Formerly it was thought
that buckwheat (*blé sarassin*) was imported into Europe from North
Africa or Palestine. However, for some years the archaeologists have
found pollen of buckwheat in northwestern Germany and at Bennekom in Gelderland, dating from the Bronze Age.[31] The last-named
village is not so far from Middelaar, so there is a probability that buckwheat has always been an indigenous plant, although it is very difficult
to distinguish between the wild and the cultivated kinds of buckwheat.[32]

The making of beer with hops was a speciality of some cities in Holland. It is an invention of the beginning of the fourteenth century.
Already in the Carolingian period hops were eaten as vegetables—for
example, in 768 in the monastery of St. Denis near Paris. The culture
of hops for industrial purposes originated in the northern provinces of
the Low Countries.[33] At the beginning of the sixteenth century the
cultivation of hops spread in England, especially in the eastern counties
of Kent, Essex, and Surrey.

One of the oldest records of the cultivation of clover is the well-

[29] R. W. K. Hinton, *The Port Books of Boston*, 1601–1640 (Lincoln Record
Society, vol. 50, 1956), pp. 23, 25, 281, 285, 315, 319, and 321.

[30] J. C. Westerman, *De rekeningen van de landscheerlijke riviertollen in
Gelderland*, 1394–95, Werken Gelre, 21 (1939), p. 231.

[31] A. Dieck, "Ueber das Alter des Buchweizenanbaues in Nordwest-deutsch-
land," in *Zeitschrift für Agrargeschichte und Agrarsoziologie*, II (1954), pp. 26–9.
A. E. van Giffen, "Een meer-perioden-heuvel, tumulus I te Bennekom, gem.
Ede," in *Bijdragen en mededelingen Gelre*, LIV (1954), pp. 17–19.

[32] J. J. Hacke-Oudemans, "Archaeologie van Bennekom," in *Een Veluws dorp*
(1958), pp. 73–5.

[33] However, in the ninth century some villeins of the abbey of Saint-Amand

known description by Sir Richard Weston of the agriculture of the Waes region, where he stayed in 1644. But already, from 1620 onwards, clover-seed was regularly imported from the Northern Netherlands into England.[34] Fattening cows with clover was recorded still earlier, in 1599, in a description of the village of Schagen in the North of Holland.[35] So it is permissible to think that this cultivation originated in the northern parts of the Low Countries too.

As research on the history of tools is only now being tackled, by Dr. van der Poel, it is still very difficult to ascertain the importance of the northern provinces in this field.[36] Probably this will prove to be considerable in butter- and cheese-making and in hay-making and hay-storage.

II

The following three *technical* problems are of interest:

1. Was intensive husbandry dependent upon the nature of the soil?

2. Were the high yields of crops (in proportion to the sowing-seed) possible before the introduction of the cultivation of fodder crops in the rotation systems? If so, how can this be explained?

3. Which fertilizers were used and in what quantities?

To answer the first question was not very difficult for the German economist, von Thünen. According to him a direct connection between the high yields of the Belgian intensive agriculture and the good quality of the soil was undeniable.[37] But his knowledge was only book-learning; he himself had never seen the agriculture of Flanders and Brabant. Quite the reverse were the opinions of those who had visited these areas. During his journey through the classic country of intensive agriculture, the Waes region, Sir Richard Weston was horrified by the "barenness of the soil," which was sandy and where "not kept in Tillage, did either produce Heath or Broom of their own natures." [38] In

---

were obliged to supply in kind malt and hops. It is possible that these two products are mentioned accidentally together: F. L. Ganshof, "Manorial organization in the Low Countries in the seventh, eighth, and ninth centuries," in *Transactions of the Royal Historical Society*, fourth series, XXXI (1949), p. 52.

[34] N. Riches, *The Agricultural Revolution in Norfolk*, p. 88. The authoress refers to the Port Books in the Public Record Office and to an unpublished article of Mrs M. A. Starr.

[35] D. A. Valcooch, *Chronijcke van Leeuwenhorn, voortijden ontrent der Sijpen gelegen in Westvrieslandt* (first ed. 1599), p. 42.

[36] For the history of some tools, see B. H. Slicher van Bath, *loc. cit.*, pp. 189–92.

[37] J. H. von Thünen, *op. cit.*, pp. 142–3.

[38] *A Discourse of Husbandrie*, pp. 5–6.

the negative, too, was the reply given to some questions of the British Board of Agriculture, reported in the introduction to Ch. Leclerc de Montlinot's "Mémoire sur la culture flamande en 1776." [39] The questions were: "Les grandes récoltes de la Flandre ne sont-elles pas dues autant à l'excellence du travail qu'à la richesse du terroir; et un laboureur flamand ne retireroit-il pas de bonnes récoltes, même d'un mauvais terrain?" ["Are not the big harvests of Flanders due as much to the excellence of the labor as to the richness of the soil; and will not a Flemish plowman draw good harvests even from a bad piece of ground?"] With some indignation, the author remarks that it is a very common prejudice in the books that the Flemish soil is unimaginably fertile. On the contrary, the quality of the soil is inferior to that in some French cantons. The high yields are obtained by unflagging zeal and by heavy fertilizing, unknown elsewhere.[40]

It is worth remarking that in England the New Husbandry was also applied first in the less fertile regions, like Norfolk, and that great successes were obtained there too.

The affirmative answer on the second question—on the possibility of high yields before the introduction of the fodder crops in the rotation system—came somewhat as a shock to me. We are so used to connecting the higher yields with the New Husbandry that it is a novel view to state the contrary. But we have the example of the results of a Frisian farmer, Rienck Hemmema, at Hitsum near Franeker, in the years from 1569 to 1573.[41] The proportions of the sowing-seed to the yield during these years were as follows:

	Wheat	Barley	Oats	Maple Peas	Blue Peas	Beans
1570	—	—	—	20	26	9·5
1571	17	11	3	16	24	8
1572	7	6	—	7·5	3	7
1573	7	10	5	5	7	2

[39] Ch. Leclerc de Montlinot, "Mémoire sur la culture flamande en 1776," edited with some observations by Fr. de Neufchâteau, in Olivier de Serres, Le théâtre d'agriculture et mesnage des champs, I (1804), pp. 183, 184.

[40] "C'est un prejugé assez répandu dans les livres que les terres de la Flandre sont d'une fertilité inconcevable; . . . Le sol de la Flandre est en général . . . inférieur à celui de quelques cantons de la France . . . on verra dans celui-ci [the Mémoire] quels soins et quelles peines se donnent les laboureurs flamands, et l'on concevra que si leur terre est productrice, ses dons sont achetés par des travaux et des engrais dont on n'a guère d'idée ailleurs."

[41] B. H. Slicher van Bath, Een Fries landbouwbedrijf in de tweede helft van de zestiende eeuw, Agronomisch-Historische Bijdragen, IV (1958), pp. 92–3.

Hemmema's yields for wheat in 1571 were as high as in 1800 on soil of a very good quality in the same region; for barley in 1571 and 1573, as high as in 1800 on soil of ordinary quality.

We can compare these figures with the proportions of the sowing-seed to the yields in England during the Middle Ages, in France, Germany, and Scandinavia in the sixteenth, seventeenth, and the eighteenth centuries.[42] On average, they are always for wheat 1:3·8—5·9; for barley 1:2·6—4·7; and for peas 1:1·7—4·0. So the results of Hemmema were much better. However, Hemmema was not unique. His high yields were equalled, even surpassed, by Robert Loder, a farmer at Harwell near Oxford in the years 1612 to 1620.[43]

. . . .

It is very difficult to reconstruct the rotation system of Hemmema. It is probable that every one-seventh or one-eighth of the land lay fallow; alternately corn and pulses were cultivated:

1st year pulse (peas, beans, or *grimang*, a mixture of peas and beans)
2nd year winter corn (wheat or barley)
3rd year pulse
4th year summer corn (barley or oats)

Robert Loder applied a two-course system:

1st year wheat   On the fallow sometimes pulses or vetches were cul-
2nd year fallow   tivated.
3rd year wheat or barley
4th year fallow

For the explanation of the high yields obtained by Hemmema and Loder we can point out two important facts: both fertilized their fields heavily and both cultivated pulse, besides corn. On Loder's farm the high yields were very clearly an obvious result of the heavy fertilizing. The importance of cultivating pulse is stressed by Hoskins for agricultural development in Leicestershire during the sixteenth and seventeenth centuries.[44]

[42] The proportions in detail in B. H. Slicher van Bath, *De Agrarische Geschiedenis van West-Europa, ca.* 500–*ca.* 1850 (1960), pp. 191–6, 307–8, 360–5.

[43] G. E. Fussell, *Robert Loder's Farm Accounts,* 1610–1620, Royal Historical Society, Camden third series, vol. LIII, 1936.

[44] W. G. Hoskins, *Essays in Leicestershire History* (1950), pp. 162–72; *idem,* "The Leicestershire Farmer in the Seventeenth Century," in *Agricultural History,* XXV (1951), pp. 10–11: 38·5 per cent to 46·0 per cent of the area of some farms were cultivated with pulse, in 1801 only 8·5 per cent; *idem,* "The Leicestershire Crop Returns of 1801," in *Studies in Leicestershire Agrarian History* (1949), p. 153.

In my opinion, it is quite possible that, in some regions, the two- or three-course system during the sixteenth and seventeenth centuries was followed by a rotation system in which pulse was an important crop. This could have been a transition phase to the rotation systems, including fodder crops. Elsewhere, convertible husbandry was perhaps a transition form.

For a historian it is a little bold to venture upon the problem of fertilizing. There are so many unknown factors concerning the quality and the quantity of manure produced by the cattle, the acquisition of fertilizers from outside the farm, the quantity put on the fields, and the frequency according to the years of harvests.[45]

We can discern two systems: one of a lighter manuring of approximately 180 to 240 cwt. per acre, sufficient for two or three harvests; the other of a very heavy manuring of approximately 560 to 720 cwt. per acre, serving for six to eight harvests. The yearly average quantity per acre is in each system about 80 cwt.

Hemmema probably used on his farm at least 560 cwt. per acre for six harvests. Robert Loder manured each year 8 or 8.5 per cent of his fields, serving for twelve years or six harvests. The quantities of manure are unknown. Neither obtained enough manure from their own cattle. Rienck Hemmema bought large quantities from the citizens of Franeker, who had their own milch-cows. Loder had manure from his sheep and pigeons; in addition, he bought malt-dust and ashes.

In the Low Countries, since the Middle Ages, there had been a struggle for fertilizers to force up the yield of the fields. The Flemish farmers had already begun in the Middle Ages to buy night-soil and town refuse. In the seventeenth century, after the extension of cole-seed culture, oilcakes from the oilmills were added to this. The ashes of wood and peat were used. Peat-ash was imported into Flanders chiefly from Holland, where peat was practically the only fuel for domestic use and for industry. Besides fertilizing with marl, which was already a very old custom in the southern provinces, the farmers came to apply a dressing of lime as well.

In the western provinces of the Low Countries, where cattle breeding was very important, the proportion of the grasslands to arable was very favourable, much better than in most parts of Europe. For each acre of arable land a large quantity of manure was available.

---

[45] Some observations on fertilizing in B. H. Slicher van Bath, "Robert Loder en Rienck Hemmema," *It beaken*, XX (1958), pp. 98–105: corrected on some points in *idem, De Agrarische Geschiedenis van West-Europa*, pp. 279–87.

III

A discussion of the *economic* conditions under which intensive agriculture developed in the Low Countries involves their whole economic life. We shall restrict ourselves here to three questions:

1. Under what regional economic circumstances did the intensive agriculture originate?
2. On what kind of farms, so far as size and ownership are concerned?
3. In which period?

Intensive agriculture in the form of higher corn yields or of the cultivation of commercial crops calls, as we have seen, for a great demand for these products, much labour, and heavy fertilizing. To create the demand and to supply the labour, a certain minimum of population density is necessary. So we shall find the intensive agriculture especially in the neighbourhood of large centres of consumption such as industrial towns and royal or princely residences.

In some cases the refuse of the towns will be used as fertilizer, but that certainly is not enough. Cattle manure is needed in increasing quantities. But decrease of fallow is, of course, a usual result of intensive agriculture, thus leaving less pasture for cattle. So, in general, agriculture can only be intensified in those regions where large natural pasture lands exist—either in mountain districts, or near the rivers or the coast.[46]

There is a reciprocal action between the rise and growth of the towns and the degree of development in the agriculture of the neighbourhood of those towns. Characteristic of the older agriculture were the rather large local differences in development. There were already in early periods islands of intensive agriculture,[47] e.g., near Lille, Bruges, Ghent, Antwerp, Alost, Brussels, probably the islands of Zeeland and South-Holland, Naaldwijk, Haarlem, Beverwijk, de Streek in West-Friesland, Franeker, etc. Likewise, in England, the counties north and east of London; in France, the Seine valley near Paris, Alsace, Provence, and Languedoc; in Germany, the Rhine valley near Worms

[46] M. Bloch, *Les caractères originaux de l'histoire rurale française,* II (ed. R. Dauvergne, 1956), p. 35.
[47] F. K. Riemann, *Ackerbau und Viehhaltung im vorindustriellen Deutschland* (1953), p. 29: "Itensitätsinseln."

and Speyer, Trier, Erfurt, Würzburg, and Augsburg; in Italy, the Po valley and in Spain, Catalonia.

In general, it is beyond dispute that the western parts of the Low Countries belonged during the sixteenth and seventeenth centuries to the most densely populated areas in Europe. Here the proportion of the urban to the total population was higher than elsewhere. Yet in detail there are still many questions left open. We have still to examine the connection between population and agriculture for many provinces. So far, this has only been done for the province of Overijssel, but there no intensified agriculture had been developed.[48] The increase of the population in Overijssel led to the development of non-agricultural employments like linen-making, peat-digging and navigation. As a result of the deficiency of manure, the arable farming could not be expanded or intensified. On the light sandy soils of Overijssel rye in particular was cultivated. The arable land was fertilized with a mixture of manure and sods of turf. The sods were cut from the commons. The arable land could not be expanded above a fixed proportion of the common waste (about 1:3 or 1:5).

Research still fails to answer the second question, regarding the size and the ownership of the farms where intensive agriculture was practised. We get the impression that the commercial crops like flax were especially cultivated on small farms, as was the case in Flanders and in Zeeland. In some parts of Overijssel flax was cultivated by the crofters. In the eighteenth century the cultivation of flax in Zeeland was shifted from the small farms to the large ones. In general, it is quite probable that most of the intensive cultivation came to be practised on small and medium-sized farms, with less than ten acres of arable land. In his *Mémoire*, Leclerc de Montlinot vehemently defends the small farms with very intensive agriculture in French Flanders against the advocates of the large farms (namely, the Physiocrats).

The small farmer and the crofter carefully weeded their land and broke up the soil with the spade. The land was worked more thoroughly than could be done with the plough in use in those days. On the larger farms the arable land could only be ploughed more deeply when the Brabant plough came into use, and that dated only from the middle of the eighteenth century.

The change-over to intensive agriculture happened in all likelihood first on the privately owned farms, though the farmer often had to

[48] B. H. Slicher van Bath, *Een samenleving onder spanning; geschiedenis van het platteland in Overijssel* (1957).

rent separate plots of land in addition to his own. The tenant-farmers did not practise a more intensive system of cultivation till later.

Still, there are other reasons why intensive agriculture will in preference be practised on the small farms. We can observe an essential difference between corn-growing and the cultivation of commercial crops. The latter is in origin horticulture, but it is horticulture transferred to the field. Horticulture, requiring much labour, is always practised on a small area. The corn-growing farms, however, are only capable of supplying corn to the market if they are of considerable size. The usual low proportion of the sowing-seed to the yield and the necessity to save a quantity of this seed for sowing the next year, as well as for feeding the farmer and his family, do not leave much over to sell. In cases of a rise in the yields, the farmers are inclined to split up the areas belonging to the farms. We can observe the same process in Ireland when potatoes became a daily food.

In cultivating comercial crops, a farmer can make a living from a very small area. A higher price can usually be obtained for these products than for cereals. Part of the commercial crops is also exported. The risk of an unsuccessful harvest with these plants is often greater than with corn-growing, but the profits to be made in successful years are far higher.

The farmers changed over so completely that they had to make use of imported cereals to provide for themselves. Only a regular supply of corn made it possible for the farmers to specialize in this manner. During the period from 1562 to 1569 the average annual grain export from the Baltic harbours to the Low Countries was 47,224 lasts of rye and 4233 lasts of wheat, together about 100,000 tons of grain. At least 13 or 14 per cent of the total consumption of grain in the Low Countries had to be met by imports.[49] In the second half of the eighteenth century the southern provinces could supply their own grain consumption—perhaps owing to the general use of potatoes for daily food. An inland province like Overijssel did not cultivate sufficient corn in the eighteenth century even for the consumption of the rural population.[50]

The third problem is a less difficult one, if we consider the history of the prices of various products. Although the prices of nearly all

[49] C. Verlinden, J. Craeybeckx and E. Scholiers, "Mouvements des prix et des salaires en Belgique au XVIe siècle," in Annales, 10 (1955), pp. 178–9. The supposed consumption per head is rather high (300 kg.); in case of a smaller consumption (240 kg.), 16·7 per cent of the total consumption had to be imported.

[50] The total population minus the urban population.

products show similar fluctuations during the same period, there is nevertheless a difference between the rise and fall of grain prices, the prices of dairy produce (cheese, butter, meat), of products from commercial crops, of industrial products, and wages. In general, the indices of the prices of agricultural products will show a relatively larger amplitude in their ups and downs than those of non-agricultural products. Among agricultural products, the indices of the prices of cereals have the sharpest fluctuations. In price-history we can discern approximately the following periods: [51]

1. c. 1310 or c. 1330 to c. 1480, the depression of the late Middle Ages, with relatively low prices for agricultural products, especially for cereals.

2. c. 1480 to 1620 or 1650, the so-called price revolution, including very high prices for grains.

3. 1620 or 1650 to 1734 or 1755, the already famous recession of the "seventeenth" century.

4. 1734 or 1755 to 1817, a rise in many prices, especially for grains.

Most of the records of intensive agriculture mentioned above belong to the periods of relatively low corn prices—the fourteenth, fifteenth, and seventeenth centuries. It was profitable to restrict in these centuries the area for corn cultivation and to apply oneself to the culture of commercial crops, or to fodder crops for increasing the number of cattle. In the sixteenth and early seventeenth centuries, and again after 1750, it was advantageous to extend the area of corn-growing and to fertilize the cornfields heavily.

During the recessions we notice mutations from arable farming to cattle breeding; during the periods of relatively high grain-prices quite the reverse happened, namely, a change-over from cattle breeding to arable farming. In the sixteenth century the farmers in Friesland and Gelderland ploughed up their grasslands. On the contrary, in the Herve region a change from arable farming to cattle breeding took place in the seventeenth and first half of the eighteenth century. After 1750 the arable land was expanded at the cost of grassland in the provinces of Groningen and East Friesland. We can observe the same process in many other countries in these periods.[52]

---

[51] In detail, B. H. Slicher van Bath, *De Agrarische Geschiedenis van West-Europa*. See also the well-known books of W. Abel, C.-E. Labrousse, F. Simiand, J. Sirol, and others.

[52] In detail, B. H. Slicher van Bath, *ibid.*

Another symptom of the sensitivity of agriculture to price relations we can observe in the extension of arable land by the reclaiming of peat-moors and impoldering and damming up land. The new polders have been reclaimed before 1644; in the period from 1665 to 1764 the average annual area is very low; after 1764 it rises again: [53]

AVERAGE AREA YEARLY RECLAIMED IN THE NETHERLANDS, 1540–1840

Period	Average Area Yearly Reclaimed, in acres	Indices 1715–1739 = 100
1540–1564	3642	346·0
1565–1589	793	75·3 (war-years)
1590–1614	3578	339·9
1615–1639	4406	418·5
1640–1664	2874	273·0
1665–1689	1218	115·7
1690–1714	1238	117·6
1715–1739	1053	100·0
1740–1764	998	94·8
1765–1789	1772	168·3
1790–1814	1567	148·8

It is self-evident that in a type of agriculture like that of the Low Countries, in which so much is aimed at production for the market, the mutations are influenced by the price relations. The periods of relatively high prices for commercial crops and for dairy produce coincide with the periods of the most intensified agriculture.

This is not in accordance with a statement by von Thünen. He suggested that the rise of the wealth of a nation and the increase of its population made a more intensive agriculture profitable.[54] As to the connection between a dense population and intensive agriculture, I believe he is right; but as for any connection with the rise of wealth, this is in my opinion questionable. The author of the often-cited *Mémoire sur la culture flamande* refers to the moral qualities of the

[53] H. Blink, *Geschiedenis van den boerenstand en den landbouw in Nederland*, II (1904), p. 112. A graph of the land dammed up from 1200 till 1950, in J. van Veen, "Grafieken van indijkingen in Nederland," in *Tijdschrift van het Koninklijk Nederlandsch Aardrijkskundig Genootschap*, 2nd ser., vol. LXV (1948), p. 23, without figures of the various periods and covering only land won from the sea, not the reclaiming of inland lakes.

[54] J. H. von Thünen, *op. cit.*, p. 262.

Flemish farmers: their industry, continuous labour, economy, and even their avarice. "On dit, avec raison, que le fermier Flamand, pour vivre, lésine sur tout, et fait argent du tout." [55]

It is not a picture of wealth, but of scarcely controlled poverty. Wealth was not the cause of the intensifying of agriculture. The cause was rather the necessity to make a living for an increased and dense population during the periods of relatively low grain prices.

THE SUPREMACY OF THE MESTA'S PASTURAGE PRIVILEGES *

Julius Klein

The Mesta, a privileged corporation embracing all the migratory sheepherders of Castile, was founded at the end of the thirteenth century by royal charter. The selection below from Julius Klein's classic but still authoritative study of this organization describes it at the height of its extraordinary powers during the reigns of Ferdinand and Isabella.

In the presence of the high court or chancillería at Valladolid, late in 1501, a distinguished attorney representing the city of Cáceres made what was for that period a truly surprising observation. With reference to certain decrees issued by Ferdinand and Isabella granting excessive grazing rights to the Mesta, he declared that "such things cannot be called just or honest, since they are not for the public good but for the private interests of a favored few!" The remark came at the close of a scathing denunciation of the royal policy of systematic repression of agriculture and sedentary sheep raising. It was daring beyond anything that had been heard in a Castilian court of justice in many a long year, coming as it did in such times of unquestioned obedience to the determined policies of the newly united monarchy of Ferdinand and Isabella. There must have been the gravest provocation to elicit a statement so dangerously near treason. A careful survey

[55] Ch. Leclerc de Montlinot, *op. cit.*, p. 202. ["It is said, rightly, that to live the Flemish farmer haggles over everything and makes money out of everything." Editor's note.]

* Reprinted by permission of the publishers from Julius Klein, *The Mesta* (Cambridge, Mass.: Harvard University Press, 1920), pp. 316–20, 325–26. Copyright, 1920, Harvard University Press.

of those policies and of their administration will reveal that there was indeed provocation for the sentiment of the attorney from Cáceres.

As in the case of the judicial and financial affairs of the Mesta, so in matters of pasturage, the accession of Ferdinand and Isabella marked the beginning of a new era in the development of the organization. Theirs was the task of laying new foundations for the agrarian life of Castile. Generations of economic confusion and political turmoil had so exhausted the country that there was dire need for almost any kind of reconstruction. A systematic programme of agricultural promotion, supplemented with plans for a diversifying sedentary pastoral industry and for forest conservation, would by no means have been beyond the capabilities of these enlightened sovereigns. It is true that geographic obstacles and social prejudices might have deterred somewhat the rapid and uniform advance of agriculture throughout Castile. Nevertheless the agrarian reforms of Charles III in the eighteenth century, achieved in the face of these very obstacles as well as of others which did not exist at the time of the Catholic Kings, inspire justifiable regrets that the newly united monarchy committed the realm so unreservedly to the large-scale migratory pastoral industry. It would be difficult indeed to exaggerate the possibilities of such a programme of agricultural development had it been carried out systematically and vigorously during the forty crucial and future-building years of this reign. Most unfortunately for the future of Castile, Ferdinand and Isabella lost no time in displaying that marked partiality toward the pastoral exploitation of their kingdoms which was to be so conspicuous throughout this period.[1] The explanation for this attitude, which was given such emphatic expression in all of their Mesta legislation, was their mercantilistic interest in promoting the source of supply for what had long been Spain's principal and almost only export commodity. It was their persistent devotion to this policy of subordinating agriculture to pasturage which forced later monarchs to confess somewhat sadly that "the exploitation and conservation of the pastoral industry is the principal sustenance of these kingdoms."[2] Every effort was made to extend pasturage, not only in Castile, but in the other parts of the peninsula. Any local attempts to improve agriculture such as took place in Murcia, and in Granada after the reconquest of that kingdom, were openly forbidden, or else choked off by prohibitive export taxes. These measures soon encouraged the entregadores to leave their beaten paths

[1] Haebler, *Wirtschaftliche Blüte Spaniens*, p. 24; Ansiaux in the *Revue d'économie politique*, June, 1893, p. 528, citing references.

[2] *Nueva Recop.*, lib. 3, tit. 14, ley 1.

in the cañadas [3] and to levy profitable fines for violations of the new laws.[4] Nor did such efforts on the part of the itinerant magistrates lack support from the monarchs. In 1489 a broadly worded royal decree was issued, authorizing the correction of cañada boundaries along the lines followed fifty years previous to that date. Armed with this document, the entregadores pushed back the boundary marks of enclosures on both sides of the sheep highways, on the pretext that the townspeople had surreptitiously altered them at some time during the past half century.[5] In some instances the death penalty was threatened by the Mesta justices if the enclosure walls were again altered.[6]

Every possible device of the new government was turned to the task of concentrating the rural energies and resources of Castile upon the sheep industry. Seldom, if ever, has the whole agrarian life of a people been held in so firm a grip or been made to follow so strictly the single-minded purpose of a determined administration. For forty years no measure was overlooked which might contribute to the desired end —a truly astonishing record of paternalism, even in an age of autocracy. The importation of wheat into Castile from Aragon was permitted in order that there should be no inducements to plant on pasture lands. Large tracts of the royal demesne in the Serena region of Estremadura and in the *montes* of Toledo were leased to the Mesta.[7] As soon as the crown had acquired control of the vast estates of the military orders arrangements were also made for the exploitation of those highly esteemed pasturage regions.[8] The activities of the indefatigable entregadores were soon supplemented by the cooperation of the corregidores, the most useful of royal administrative agents, and of the special judge-inquisitor (*juez pesquisidor*), that favorite device of the new autocracy. These inquisitors were usually royal counsellors of the highest rank, whom Mesta members soon found to be most efficacious in restricting and even breaking down the enclosures of the more important towns, monasteries, and military orders.[9]

The famous reform Cortes held at Toledo in 1480, instead of in-

[3] [Special overland highways for the migrating sheep flocks. Editor's note.]
[4] Arch. Mesta, A–3, Albacete, 1487 ff.
[5] *Concordia de 1783*, ii, fol. 303.
[6] Arch. Mesta, A–1, Albertura, 1495; A–1, Azeluche, 1497 ff. It is interesting to note that Morisco peasants were frequently mentioned as the defendants in suits regarding the extension of arable land into the cañadas.
[7] Arch. Simancas, Patronato Real, 1064 (1479); Clemencín, *Elógio*, p. 155.
[8] *Bull. Ord. Milit. Alcant.*, *pp.* 263, 457.
[9] Arch. Mesta, C–10, Cuenca, 1477 ff.: a series of mandates of such a *juez pesquisidor* after an investigation of the highland pastures above Cuenca, which fed, at that time, nearly 500,000 sheep.

sisting upon the curtailment of the Mesta's pasturage privileges, as
has been alleged,[10] took precisely the opposite stand. The deputies
obediently concurred with the anounced policies of the monarchs by
commanding the evacuation of all parts of town commons which had
been preempted by local officials for their personal uses during the
recent period of misrule under Henry IV.[11] This measure was soon
followed up, not only by more general legislation guaranteeing the
rights of the Mesta in the common pastures,[12] but also by making examples of a few of the larger cities which still dared to put on bold
fronts against the pastoral policy of the new monarchy. In 1491 the city
of Ávila was commanded to nullify its new ordinances which had permitted the sale and enclosure of parts of the local commons.[13] In the
same year the spread of agriculture in the recently reconquered parts
of the kingdom of Granada was sharply checked by an edict forbidding
enclosures unless specially licensed by the crown.[14] Even when royal li-
censes permitting enclosures were granted, the towns were ordered to
rent such enclosed fields for pastoral purposes at least part of the time.[15]
The old "five forbidden things" (cosas vedadas)—the orchards, grain
fields, vineyards, ox pastures, and mown meadows—were still to be re-
spected by the Mesta; but in each instance evidence must be forthcoming, in case of doubt, that these enclosures were actually being used
for the purposes designated. The lack of such evidence would mean
the immediate removal of barriers and the admission of the migrant
flocks; and the entregadores were ever ready, not only to prove the
absence of any justification for the enclosures, but to absolve the herdsmen from any blame or charges, save for actual damage done when
their animals trespassed.

Among other devices to place more town lands at the disposal of
the Mesta herds was the encouragement of the hoja system of cultivation. Under this arrangement a section or hoja of cultivated land was
left fallow each year, and was therefore available for pasturage and
fertilization by the passing flocks. Mediaeval Castilian agriculture had
never become sufficiently extensive or important to develop an active
and methodically administered three-field system. There had, however,

[10] Hume, Spanish People, p. 276.
[11] Nueva Recop., lib. 7, tit. 7, ley 3.
[12] Ramirez, Pragmáticas del Reyno, fols. lxii–lxiii: decrees of 1489 and after,
enforcing the measures of 1480.
[13] Ramirez, op. cit., fol. cxlviii; Jordana, Voces Forestales, p. 133.
[14] Nueva Recop., lib. 7, tit. 7, leyes 10, 11, 13.
[15] Arch. Ayunt. Cáceres, Docs. Isabel, no. 30: a royal permit of 1488 allowing
the leasing of such enclosures.

been more or less irregular practices regarding the leaving of untilled strips (*entrepanes*), resembling the English balks, between the *panes* or grain fields. Isabella was keenly interested in the pastoral possibilities of these untilled *entrepanes* and the fallow *hojas*, and did much, through instructions to corregidores and various other officials, to encourage these agricultural practices.[16] In a word, the constant purpose was clearly to check any shrinkage of local pasturage which might interfere with the migratory sheep industry.

. . . .

All of these measures had their desired effects. They gave extraordinary powers to the sheep owners and the Mesta; they made the pastoral industry unquestionably supreme over all other forms of rural life throughout the realm. The first decades of the sixteenth century saw the Spanish wool trade at the zenith of its activity. Within ten years after the death of Ferdinand, the Mesta had added almost 1,000,-000 sheep to its already numerous flocks, so that by 1526 nearly 3,500,000 merinos were availing themselves of the liberal privileges accorded to them by the monarchy. This was the heritage of the agrarian policy of Ferdinand and Isabella. Eminently successful in the accomplishment of its immediate object, it expanded the pastoral industry out of all proportion to the other productive activities of the country, and on a scale which was not to be surpassed elsewhere for three hundred years. With all these determined plans, however, there were planted the seeds whence sprang that hopeless tangle of economic sophistry which later completely choked off the normal development of the country's rural resources. One of the larger roots of the evil growth which strangled not only the agrarian life of Castile but also the political morale of the country goes back directly to the triumphs of the pastoral policy of Ferdinand and Isabella.

THE KING'S PROCEEDINGS *

Maurice Beresford

At the same time that the flocks of the Mesta were undergoing a tremendous expansion, there was a large-scale shift in England from

[16] Arch. Mesta, R–1, Rabanos, 1496; B–2, Barco, 1502 ff.

* From Maurice Beresford, *The Lost Villages of England* (London: Lutterworth Press, 1954), pp. 102–106, 178–82. Reprinted by permission of the publishers.

arable farming to sheep raising. It is interesting to compare the latter with the Spanish experience. Note particularly the contrast between Ferdinand and Isabella's "truly astonishing record of paternalism" in favour of the Mesta and the English monarchy's concern over the depopulating effect of enclosure and "the greediness of Graziers and Sheepmasters." Maurice Beresford is Professor of Economic History at the University of Leeds.

I

Before 1489 it would have been difficult to argue in an English court of law that enclosure was an offence proscribed by statute. There was the Statute of Merton of 1235, a time when villages and fields were still growing. The statute was directed against men who encroached upon the common pastures and wastes as they drove their expanding arable fields outwards from the village. Appropriate as a restrictive influence in a period of colonisation, it was not fitted to justify action against those who were attacking those very arable fields in the advancing movement of grass against corn in later centuries.

John Rous,* who disapproved of enclosure, claimed that he had presented a petition to Parliament asking for legislation in 1459. Even earlier there is the petition from the village of Chesterton to the Parliament of 1414 anticipating many later stories of the shepherd and his dog inheriting the empty village fields:

there was made great waste in the same Manor . . . of housing—that is to say of halls and chambers and other houses of office that were necessary in the same manor—and none housing left standing there but if it were a sheepcote or a barn or swine-sty and a few houses beside to put in beasts.[1]

But no general prohibition resulted until 1489.

Individual citizens who were aggrieved by depopulating enclosure might have found their way to the common law courts or to Chancery to obtain redress. Such cases seem to be few, but since the fifteenth-century records are poorly calendared and indexed this verdict may some day be upset. There are a few cases in Chancery between 1485 and 1517 in which individuals present petitions alleging damage from depopulating enclosure, but before 1489 they had no statute to

* John Rous (d. 1491) was a member of the clergy and author of *Historia Regum Angliae*. He compiled lists of villages depopulated by enclosure. [Editor's note.]

[1] R.P., iv, p. 60.

plead their support. The Chancery Petitions of this kind, such as that of the inhabitants of Shuckburgh, were concerned only with the fact that legal rights of common had been usurped. They strove to assert rights, rather than base their case on a view that depopulation is illegal by statute or contrary to the welfare of the commonwealth. We find the same inhabitants proceeding against their depopulating land-lord in the Court of Requests; and there are cases in Star Chamber, and also indirect evidence that the Council of the North was also used by aggrieved villagers. These individuals had been fortunate enough to obtain access to a court in defence of their property rights. Many of the dispossessed could not have hoped for such redress: the sole owner of a lordship peopled by tenants-at-will might find little more than a shadowy custom to restrain him, and during the Wars of the Roses many customs as well as laws had been effectively silenced.[2]

The motive for the first intervention by the Crown was not the defence of individual property rights, but the fear of danger to the State if depopulation were allowed to continue. It is significant that the Act of 1489 was preceded by a similar measure for the Isle of Wight alone. The chalklands of the island were attractive to graziers, but shepherds and sheep pastures seemed to endanger military security. These fears are expressed in the preamble to the Act of 1488.

It is to the surety of the Realm of England that the Isle of Wight . . . be well inhabited with English people . . . the which Isle is late decayed of people by reason that many Towns and Villages be let down and the field dyked and made pastures for beasts and cattles. The same Isle . . . is desolate and not inhabited but occupied with beasts and cattle, so that if hasty remedy be not provided that Isle cannot be long kept and defended but open and ready to the hands of the King's enemies, which God forbid.

The Act did not mention sheep specifically, and it is curious that although pasture is mentioned as the root of the evil, the Act did not make conversion an offence. Penalties were to be imposed only if hold-ings were taken into one man's hands so that total value exceeded ten marks a year:

many dwelling places farms and farmholds have of late times been used to be taken into one mens' hold and hands, that of old time were wont to be in many several persons' holds and hands.

No new machinery for discovering offenders or levying fines was

[2] Shuckburgh: C1/445/51; Requests 2/8/339; Council of the North: D.R.O. (Y.), R.As. 20/5.

set up, and I have not been able to trace any enforcement of the Act. We have only a Proclamation of February 1492/93 in admonitory terms. Nor does there seem to have been any serious attempt to enforce the general Statute of 1489 until after the supplementary Act of 1515. Polydore Vergil, looking back from 1534, gave no hint of vigorous enforcement. For him these were years when

the abuses were not checked early in their development, and afterwards they hardened and became more durable.[3]

The general Statute of 1489 was principally directed against the offence, not of engrossing (as in the Isle of Wight Act), but of depopulation. It was the decay of "houses of husbandry" which created an offence. Such a house was one which had with it 20 acres of land "normally" (that is, for three years past) under the plough. Until these houses were rebuilt, the overlord of the offender was permitted to take half the profits of the holding as a penalty, the other half falling to the Crown. The assumption was that overlords would take action. In fact the identity of interest between overlord and an enclosing tenant seems to have been close enough to prevent any action. The main interest of this Act lies in its preamble, with its long description of the ills attending depopulation.

Great inconvenience daily doth increase by desolation and pulling down and wilfull waste of houses and Towns within this his realm, and laying to pasture lands which customarily have been used in tillage, whereby idleness —ground and beginning of all mischiefs—daily doth increase, for where in some Towns two hundred persons were occupied and lived by their lawful labours, now be there occupied two or three herdmen and the residue fallen in idleness; the husbandry, which is one of the greatest commodities of the realm, is greatly decayed; churches destroyed; the service of God withdrawn; the bodies there buried not prayed for; the patron and curate wronged; the defence of this land against our enemies outwards feebled and impaired: to the great displeasure of God, to the subversion of the policy and good rule of this land.[4]

. . . .

Government interest in the restraint of enclosure did not become active again until 1514, when two drafts were prepared for the Council. In the preamble of the first, a Bill, the blame was thrown on town investors and speculators who were buying up land to enclose it for pasture.

---

[3] Polydore Vergil, ed. D. Hay, Camden Soc., lxxiv (1950), pp. 277–9.
[4] 4 Henry VII c. 6 (1488); c. 19 (1489).

Many merchant adventurers, clothmakers, goldsmiths, butchers, tanners and other artificers and unreasonable covetous persons do encroach many more farms than they are able to occupy. Farms and ploughs are decayed . . . and no more parishioners in many parishes but a neat-herd and a shepherd.[5]

The same theme is stated in the draft Proclamation.

[There is] scarcity of grain by converting and engrossing [by those who] for their own lucre neglecteth tillage.

The Act of 1515, made perpetual in 1516, concentrated upon the offence of conversion from tillage to pasture: land which was tillage in February 1515 was to remain so, or to be turned back to the plough if it had been converted.[6] As in 1489, failure involved forfeit of half profits, but if the overlord was not zealous in the cause of the common-wealth then the next superior lord could seize.

II

It was the failure of this zeal which helps to explain the Commissions of Inquiry set up by Wolsey in 1517 to investigate offences up and down the country, and the supplementary Inquiry of 1518. From the facts found, the Crown could set an example by suing for half profits from its own tenants.

. . . .

We can see in a number of ways that everyone assumed grazing to be a more profitable use for the enclosed land than corn. One of the tasks of the Commission of 1517 was to ascertain any increase in value which had followed enclosure. The old and new values were set down in many of their returns and substantial increases can be seen.[7] The very legislation which first set itself to discourage depopulating en-closure sought a remedy in taking away the profits of any conversion. Half the profits were to be forfeit. We have seen how the Crown began in 1538 to follow this same course in proceeding for half profits against tenants other than its own. The same course was followed by Hales in 1548 when he suggested a tax of a penny on sheep in the common fields and 2*d.* on ewes and lambs in several pasture, with 1½*d.* on other sheep in enclosed pasture. Such a tax was enacted in

---

[5] *L.P.H.*, iv (iii), no. 5750.
[6] 6 Henry VIII c. 5; 7 Henry VIII c. 1.
[7] Text of the articles of Inquiry in *T.P.*, i, p. 41, where the strong continuity with 1517 will be seen.

1549, only to be repealed soon after (although evidence of its collection has been found) as "unworkable." [8]

The greater profits of enclosed land were indeed used by some enclosers as a defence. One argued that it enabled him to pay the Crown more rent; another, Belknap, that it had considerably augmented the yield for the incumbent from acres of glebe no longer in tillage. The willingness to pay fines and buy pardons looks as if men thought they could nevertheless recoup themselves.

At Wormleighton the rents had been raised from eight to thirteen pounds when the fields went down to pasture. Spencer's petition against reconversion stressed how the Crown as superior landlord had gained. He also described the hundred pounds which he had spent on a new manor house and on refurnishing the church. But the jury had found that the value of the lands had risen from forty to sixty pounds a year. To spend five years' increment on capital betterment was not so philanthropic as it looked.[9]

When the anti-stapler pamphleteer [10] wrote his *Treatise* concerning *the Staple* (c. 1533–36) he was not one to deny that the enclosers followed a profitable course. When he wrote that

for the less profit they destroyed the more

he had ceased to think in terms of money profits. He was in the realm of social advantage and welfare economics. The "more profit" destroyed was the social asset of having villagers—

in one village to destroy the labours and living of a 400 or a 500 of common people.

The conflict between private benefit and social benefit which this pamphleteer expressed can be put no more clearly than in the words with which Hales encouraged the jury of 1548. He set three opposites balanced against each other, and the last of these pairs was "commonwealth" and "private profit:"

for God, the King and the commonwealth, if ye serve them truly and faithfully, as they be able to defend you against the Devil, the world and private profit, so may you be sure they will suffer no person to do you injury.

In the diagnosis of enclosers' motives in the *Discourse* and in

---

[8] 1565: E 159/357 Mich. m. 523 ff.; E 178/424. Consequent prosecutions may be represented by E 159/357 Mich. m. 395 and E 159/358 Trin. m. 107.

[9] 1607: C 205/5/1–6: Leics. membranes published by L. A. Parker in *T.L.A.S.*, xxiii; for Northants. proceedings at the Assizes of 1609 see E 163/19/8.

[10] Warws. returns in *D.I.*, pp. 456–66.

Hales' *Defence,* the leading theme is human greed. It was the theme of Rous, More, Crowley, and Latimer.

The Council saw what hurt had grown . . . if the greediness of Graziers and Sheepmasters were not in time resisted.

Covetousness must be attacked at the roots, he urged. The roots were the relative profitability of grass against corn:

who will maintain husbandry which is the nurse of every County as long as sheep bring so great gain? who will be at the cost to keep a dozen in his house to milk kine, make cheese, carry it to the market when one poor soul may by keeping sheep get him a greater profit . . . who will not be contented for to pull down houses of husbandry so that he may stuff his bags full of money?

It will be noticed that the sheep is considered to be more profitable than kine because of its low labour costs. How much greater the advantage of sheep over corn when it came to labour costs!

When the characters in the *Discourse* came to argue the causation of "enclosure" they were concerned with more than one sense of that word, and the author took pains to show he did not object to enclosure which took away no one's rights:

I mean not all Inclosures . . . but only of such Inclosures as turneth commonly arable fields into pastures

says the Doctor, and he then turns to his programme for halting and reversing the conversion to grass:

as long as they find more profit by pasture than by tillage they will still inclose.

They see there is most advantage in grazing and breeding than in husbandry and tillage by a great deal. And so long as it is so, the pasture shall ever encroach upon the tillage for all the laws that ever can be made to the contrary.

and in reply to the Knight's request for a practical solution the Doctor says:

to make the profit of the plough to be as good . . . rate for rate, as the profit of the graziers and sheepmasters . . . either make as little gains to grow by pastures as there groweth by tillage; or else make that there may grow as much profit by tillage as did before by pastures.

We must understand that all things ought not to be forced or constrained by the penalties of the law, but some so, and others by allurements and rewards rather.

The husbandman supports the Doctor with a story of a neighbour who twelve years earlier had found that

profit was but small by the ploughs . . . and turned either part or all of the arable ground into pasture and thereby waxed very rich. . . .

In the third dialogue the Doctor returns to his policy of discouraging sheep and encouraging the plough:

I showed before that there is more lucre by grazing of ten acres to the occupier alone than is in tillage of twenty and the causes thereof be many. One is that grazing requires small charge and small labour which in tillage consumes much of the master's gain.

and the Doctor concludes by summarising the policy to follow for curing a society sick with the plague of avarice. Money had tempted men to convert to grass, and with money they should be tempted back to corn-growing:

with lucre they should be enticed to occupy the plough, yea and with other privileges.

There is no doubt that Hales was in full agreement with John Rous that the cornfields had been abandoned because of the greater income from sheep farming.

SUGGESTIONS FOR ADDITIONAL READING

Joan Thirsk, *Tudor Enclosures*. Historical Association Pamphlet No. G 41 (London, 1959).

AN EYEWITNESS'S ACCOUNT OF A SEVENTEENTH-CENTURY ENCLOSURE *

W. H. Hosford

This interesting account drawn from contemporary sources shows that by the seventeenth century there were enclosures for improved farming, as well as for sheep raising. Caythorpe thus anticipates the

* From *The Economic History Review*, 2nd Series, Vol. IV, No. 2 (1951). Reprinted by permission of The Economic History Society and the author.

*type of enclosure more commonly associated with the eighteenth
century. W. H. Hosford has taught at the University of Notting-
ham.*

In the course of a search of the parish chest at Caythorpe (Kesteven, Lincolnshire)[1] a remarkable document in seventeenth-century
handwriting came to light. This proved to be an account of the enclosure of the parish in the 1650's, written by the then rector, the Rev.
Ralph Tunstall. So full an account of such an early enclosure, written
by one who was both an eye-witness and a participant, must be unique,
or nearly so, and the story, incidentally, gives a human-interest picture
of life in a Lincolnshire parish 300 years ago.

The enclosure has a number of unusual features. For instance, it
was a very early example of the kind of enclosure more typical of the
eighteenth century—it was not an enclosure for sheep-farming—and
many of the features of the procedure of the later parliamentary enclosures are shown to go back at least to the 1650's. The larger farmers
were the promoters of the scheme—the lord of the manor was at first,
and for a long time, opposed to it. The narrative reveals the strength
of the moral and religious feeling against enclosure and a superstitious
belief in ill-luck attending landowners who enclosed their commons.
Above all, the story provides a striking example of the dangers of enclosure by agreement without parliamentary confirmation.

The following summary is based mainly on the original narrative
but partly on other sources of information that the writer has been
able to trace. Unless otherwise stated, the information is derived from
the narrative.

In the middle of the seventeenth century the manor of Caythorpe
was owned by the Earl of Suffolk but let on a long lease to Sir Edward
Hussey. Possibly as a result of the cost of the erection and maintenance
of "that noble pallace" at Audley End, the earl was in financial difficulties and offered to sell all the land he owned in the manor. Sir Edward refused to buy any,[2] but most of the farmers of the village bought
their own holdings—and the Husseys were left only with the land in
their own occupation. By 1650, therefore, we find Caythorpe in the

---

[1] Made by the Rector of Caythorpe (the Rev. A. J. Ison) and the present
writer, for documents that would illustrate the lectures in connexion with an adult
education class held in the village under the auspices of the University of Notting-
ham, Department of Adult Education.

[2] He had been fined £8750 for his part in the Civil War, and the family were
pressed for money.

exceptional situation of being a village mainly owned by small, or fairly small, freeholders.

The "principall Freeholders" (i.e. the larger farmers) now began agitating to have the parish of Caythorpe enclosed, "being weary of the drudgery & charge, & much other uneasiness of the way of husbandry by tillage; & chiefly by a prospect of improving their estates." They pressed for an enclosure with the utmost determination, and in spite of the opposition of the smaller farmers and cottagers, who believed that an enclosure would result in great damage to them—although their farms and cottages might be much improved in value "yet it was not that alone by which they maintained ther famelys, but ther labour, through much imployment, which uppon inclosure must fall; & ther livlihood together. But they had neither purses nor stomack to make a vigorous opposition against those who were every way better furnished to carry on ther designe; & therefore sate still, & submitted."

It was necessary for the promoters of the enclosure to obtain the consent of the lord of the manor; this was now a Mr. Edward Hussey, a younger son of Sir Edward—who had died in 1648. Mr. Hussey was opposed to the enclosure and, in spite of continued pressure, refused to agree to it—mainly because he would derive little benefit from it, having no common rights. The larger farmers were so determined to secure enclosure, however, that they took advice and in order to embarrass Hussey they started a legal action about a disputed sheep-walk, "whereupon the Lawyers, forseeing that it might be made a peice of work which might turne to ther account, ther being a purse on ye one part and stomack on ye other, they thought it adviseable not to make an end at one Tryall, and they found an occasion of a nonsute which could beget some more work for them, not omitting to encourage both partys to go on." The promoters of the enclosure soon found the legal expenses very heavy, and they endeavoured to make the whole village contribute to the cost. The smaller farmers and labourers naturally objected, but they were forced to pay because the promoters appointed spies to watch for the least trespass on the part of any of the dissenters and threatened that every such trespass would be followed by a legal action, which would be more expensive than the contribution—"so by this means all were brought in."

All this led to great confusion in the village, and the matter was the common talk of the county, but eventually Edward Hussey, who was then about 28 years of age, was persuaded by his mother and by a Mr. Knight, a trustee of the estate, to agree to an enclosure—on the ground that although the "improvment would not be very great as is usyall in other Ldships; yet it would be an improvment." In the course of this discussion it transpired that Hussey's reluctance was in part due to a belief that it was very unlucky for lords to enclose—"I am possest with a strong conceit that after all is finished I shall not live long to enjoy it," and he proceeded to mention several landowners who had enclosed their commons and had died soon after. However, he was laughed out of this "superstitious conceit (as they cald. it)" and the enclosure went forward. Commissioners were chosen—some representing the lord of the manor and some the other freeholders— surveyors were appointed and articles drawn up and agreed to. Mr. Hussey "was ready to purchase all the land in ye parish that any were ready to sell and gave the highest prices . . . for he was minded to sell any lands he had elsewhere & to lay out ye money in this parish together where he meant to erect a famely." Misfortune, however, dogged the work of enclosure: a Mr. Colson, who had been Hussey's principal advisor in the matter, died suddenly; then one of the commissioners died suddenly; next another commissioner fell ill and "being afrighted by the fate of ye 2 former, writ to Mr. Hussey to excuse him from acting, & he recovered."

The remaining commissioners continued with the work, the land was surveyed and re-divided, and the freeholders proceeded to dig out their ditches and plant their quicksets, when a "prodigious accident unforseen and unsuspected happened to embarrass their designes." "Forasmuch" (continues the reverend narrator) "as they never consulted with God, nor his most Holy laws of equity and justice, but trusted to ther own wisdome & ye counsell of the lawyers, ye Ld. gave them an instance of his power and displeasure; laying such a block in ther way as not only threw it into great confusion but also cost them deare to remove it." This unforeseen accident was the death, after an illness of eight days, of Edward Hussey—"as he prophetically had prognosticated." He was succeeded as lord of the manor by his brother Charles (afterwards Sir Charles, and a Knight of the Shire for Lincolnshire), but there was some delay over proving the will. When this matter was cleared up it was found that all the transfers of land in connexion with the enclosure had been legally completed except a piece belonging to a Captain Thorold and two oxgangs belonging to a Richard Seymor. Edward Hussey had agreed to buy Seymor's land at its post-enclosure value, but Charles Hussey refused to pay more than the much lower pre-enclosure price. Captain Thorold now stepped in and bought Seymor's land and he was a man who "knew how to make his owne terms for his land or break the Inclosure." He put his plough into Seymor's land, ploughing through hedges and ditches, and he put his cattle into the enclosed fields that occupied the site of what would have been the fallow field. The freeholders complained to Mr. Hussey, but his answer was that "he was well content that ye Inclosure should be throwne in, & if the estate had fallen to him before it was begun it should never have been as long as he should live, yet seeing it was gone so far, he would not oppose it, nevertheless he could not be concerned, nor be at any charge to defend it; but leave it wholly to themselves to deale with Mr. Thorold as the counsell should advise." The freeholders now brought an action against Captain Thorold, but they failed, and eventually, after prolonged negotiations, they appear to have paid Thorold some £300 more for the land than it was worth. This amount was raised by a tax on the land of the village, each free-holder (except the lord of the manor) paying in proportion to the amount of land held.

According to the narrative their troubles and obstructions were now at an end "and this is the present state of Caythorpe and Freiston since the enclosure concluded An.Do. 1658." The writer is not quite correct in his date, for in 1664 the enclosure agreements had not yet been confirmed by a Decree in Chancery, as was usual in such cases. On 26 May of that year certain of the freeholders of Caythorpe presented a bill of complaint in the Court of Chancery against Sir Charles Hussey, the Rev. Ralph Tunstall and other freeholders, in which they set forth the main features of the enclosure agreement of "about the year 1657" in some detail. They asserted that, although this was done by the free and voluntary approbation and consent of all parties concerned, and although the complainants had accepted the lands allotted to them and had hedged and ditched and fenced them, yet the defendants denied the said agreement and inclosure and refused to accept the several plots so allotted to them respectively and had endeavored to overthrow the agreement and inclosure, "whereunto the Defendant Sir Charles Hussey by answear saith that he doth not apprehend that the said Inclosure would have beene any advantage to the said Edward Hussey or wilbe to him the said Defendant . . . but in regard that he doth conceive it will be a great advantage and improvement to the rest of the Defendants and other the Freeholders Plaintiffs he is contented and doth agree to the same." The agreement was finally confirmed by a Decree in Chancery, 27 June 1664.[3]

.   .   .   .

Even this was not quite the last stage of the enclosure. The parish of Caythorpe, which includes the hamlet of Frieston, is a long and narrow oblong; the western portion consists of heavy clay—the Low Fields; to the east of the village is the steep escarpment locally known as the "Cliff;" at the top of the cliff was the heathland—a part of Lincoln Heath, in those days a wild and uncultivated stretch of rough pasturage extending for many miles. A short distance from the edge of the Cliff was an ancient trackway known as Pottergate and the eastern boundary of the parish was formed by the old Roman road Ermine Street—locally known as the High Dyke. At the enclosure there were special provisions concerning the heathland between Pottergate and High Dyke. The northern part of this area had been bought by Edward Hussey, but the southern part had been allocated to a number of smaller freeholders. The provisions relating to the southern part are as follows:

And that all the other groundes allotted and assigned to the severall other Freeholders vppon the said Heath between Pottergate and the High Dike or Streete Banke be eaten and depastured with sheepe onely by the Freeholders whoe are owners of Plottes or Lande there. And that there be allowed the proporcion of Foure & Twenty Sheepe to every Twenty Acres and that noe Sheepe or other Stock be putt on or kept there betweene Martinmas & our Lady day. And that the aforesaid be not encreased nor altered nor any ground betweene Pottergate & the High Dike be plowed or . . . ? vpp without the consent of the Major part of the Owners of the said Grounds there and that all the said grounds vppon the Heath allotted to the freeholders aforesaid betweene the (High Dike) and Pottergate be vsed & held in severalty & vncomonable by the severall & respective Owners to whom the same should be allotted. . . . And that the Gorse and Bracken groweing or being vppon the said Heath shall from time to time be for the vse & benefitt of the person or persons their heires & assignes onely vppon whose groundes plottes or allotmentes the same shall att any time growe or be free from any blayme of Common by any other person there.

In 1761 this southern part of the heathland between Pottergate and the High Dyke was divided into fifty plots, amounting in all to 547 acres, and owned by fifteen persons. By an agreement of 3 November

[3] Sir Charles had intended to "have all things establisht by an Act of Parliament" but he died (December 1664) before this could be done.

of that year this land was redivided into fifteen plots and all restrictions were abolished.

What were the results of the enclosure? The reference to the anticipated decline in employment shows that the smaller farmers and cottagers assumed that the purpose of the intended enclosure was sheep farming—the conversion of arable into pasture. This was the predominant type of enclosure in the earlier part of the century and it usually involved the demolition of houses, and even of whole villages. The Hearth Tax returns for 1665–6 have survived and show that nothing of the sort happened at Caythorpe, there being fifty-nine houses in the parish some eight years after the re-distribution of the holdings[4]—about the same as the total number of homesteads, houses, and cottages mentioned in the key to the enclosure map.

The enclosure did not destroy the small freeholders in Caythorpe; as a result of the sale of Lord Suffolk's lands they must have been more numerous there than in most places. A survey made in 1603,[5] after naming thirty-six tenants of the Earl of Suffolk in Caythorpe and Frieston, and also a number of tenants in several other villages, states "Item there is verie little Freeholde grounde in none of theis Townes." After the enclosure of 1657 there were fifty-five freeholders owning not less than one acre in the parish—thirty-five at least were resident there—and their occupations were as follows:

Baronets, knights	2	Gentlemen	2
Blacksmith	1	Labourers	4
Carpenter	1	Mason	1
Chandler	1	Tailor	1
Clergymen	2	Weaver	1
Felmonger	1	Yeomen	29

Others (infants, occupation not recorded) 9

A comparison of the list of freeholders given in the Chancery documents of 1664 with the Hearth Tax returns of 1665–6 [6] proves that at that period about 68 per cent of the householders of the parish owned some land. A contemporary document in the estate office at Prestwold [7] shows that in some year between 1713 and 1716 (inclusive) there were forty-seven freeholders in Caythorpe parish possessing more than one

[4] Information kindly supplied by Miss F. E. Thurlby, of the Foster Library, Lincoln.

[5] Now in the Essex County Record Office.

[6] Now in the Essex County Record Office.

[7] Kindly lent to the writer by the Hon. Lady Packe.

acre, and a tithe assessment of 1846 proves that in that year there were still forty-six. It seems very possible, therefore, that the land of Caythorpe was divided among more freeholders in 1846 than in 1603!

Although the small freeholders continued to flourish it is probable that the enclosure was injurious to the poorer people of the parish. If any of them had cows they had already lost the use of certain common grounds that were sold by the Earl of Suffolk (perhaps illegally) before the enclosure was even mooted. With the enclosure of the heathland they lost not only the remaining common pasturage but also the free fuel that had been available to them. It is unfortunate that no more definite information is available concerning the effect of the enclosure on the wage-earning population of the village.

The male line of the Caythorpe Husseys died out in 1730, when the manor passed to the Pochins, and later (1804) to the Packes. On the death of Sir Edward Hussey Packe in 1946 all the family property in Caythorpe (amounting to 2200 acres) was sold. A farm institute connected with the Kesteven County Council occupies much of the land in the south heath that was governed by special provisions at the time of the original enclosure. As for Caythorpe Hall from which Sir Charles Hussey used to ride forth as a knight of the shire for Lincolnshire, this was rebuilt in 1823–4 and in 1947 was bought by a timber merchant for the sake of the trees in the park. The house and grounds have since been re-sold to a former Labour parliamentary candidate who runs the estate as a farm with TT cattle, pedigree pigs, and thousands of head of poultry. "Other days, other ways," indeed!

THE "AGRICULTURAL REVOLUTION" IN ENGLISH HISTORY: A RECONSIDERATION *

G. E. Mingay

This article, which repays careful reading, compares the old idea of the Agricultural Revolution, popular during the first two decades of this century and still perpetuated in some texts, with a summary of the

* From *Agricultural History*, Vol. 37, No. 3 (1963). Reprinted by permission of The Agricultural History Society and the author.

main conclusions drawn from subsequent research. These, as will be
seen, have considerably revised earlier interpretations. G. E. Mingay
has been a visiting professor at the University of Wisconsin and
Lecturer in Economic History at the London School of Economics and
Political Science. He is currently teaching at the University of Kent at
Canterbury.

"Revolution" is a word which has gone much out of fashion in the
popular terminology of economic history. To talk nowadays of "revolution" is to risk being considered a dangerous reactionary, or at least
an incautious obscurantist. Indeed, it is clear from the scholarly preference for "accelerated pace of economic development" or "quickening
of the growth process," that no matter how cumbrous the alternative
we must eschew the convenience of "revolution"—overlooking, incidentally, that the dictionary has it that revolutionary changes need only
be radical and need not be sudden.

The old idea of an Agricultural Revolution ran parallel, and indeed
was closely associated with that of an Industrial Revolution. Both
were once seen as remarkable inter-related changes in the methods,
organisation, and levels of production which took place in a relatively
short period of some seventy years between 1760 and 1830. For a long
time now, however, the process of industrial change has been seen as
extending much further back—some would say to the sixteenth century
—and seen also as reaching forward, to at least the later ninetenth
century; and many would pitch on the middle years of the nineteenth
century as the most vital period of development. The "agricultural
revolution" has undergone a rather similar if less severe stretching
process. Its roots in the seventeenth century, and even earlier, are now
well established, and as with industrialisation, many authorities would
place the period of most significant technical change in the middle
nineteenth century, not long before the Great Depression (another term
whose days are numbered?) swept away the old order of things
and changed fundamentally the character and emphasis of English
farming.

The traditional story of the Agricultural Revolution placed its
crucial stages firmly in the later eighteenth and early nineteenth
centuries, and the revolutionary character of the changes of that period
was thought to spring from two developments: first, the original work
of a number of pioneers whose names have become almost canonical
in the textbooks, and by whom the inefficiency of existing farming

methods was greatly modified—that celebrated quartet of agriculturists, Tull, Townshend, Coke, and Bakewell; and secondly, the large-scale enclosure of open fields by private Acts of Parliament, which not only made possible the adoption of improved farming methods but radically changed the agrarian structure, driving out small farmers and cottagers who lived out a comfortably static existence by farming mainly for subsistence, and replacing them with enterprising capitalist farmers who produced for the market.

I

The eighteenth-century innovations and the enclosure movement thus stood at the core of the old idea of the Agricultural Revolution, and it is illuminating to examine, if only very briefly, the basis from which this interpretation of English agricultural history derived. In the main, it depended on two major works, Lord Ernle's *English Farming Past and Present*, first published in 1912, and J. L. and Barbara Hammond's *The Village Labourer*, which appeared in the same year. Both books, of course, soon acquired a great reputation; the one came to be recognised as the single standard work for English agricultural history, and still has not been dislodged from this pedestal after half a century; the other has largely determined the interpretation of the social changes in the countryside, and has stamped on the minds of countless teachers and students an apparently indelible picture of social disintegration involving the exploitation by the few of the mass of humble peasantry.

Now, the influence achieved by these two works is in some ways very curious. Lord Ernle's classic was in many respects ill-balanced and defective when it first appeared, and the passage of time merely made it the more so, for in the later editions little or no effort was made to repair the omission of important contributions such as those of Tawney, Gonner, Clapham, and even the Hammonds. Ernle used, in fact, only the sources with which he was thoroughly familiar—particularly the contemporary farming books of Arthur Young, William Marshall and the reports of the Board of Agriculture—and he ignored the local histories, topographical writings, diaries, and publications of record societies that were available in his time.[1] In short, his was a book based almost entirely on a partial selection of secondary sources, and

---

[1] Lord Ernle, *English Farming Past and Present* (6th ed.; Chicago: Quadrangle Books, 1961), Introduction by G. E. Fussell, p. xxii.

it was especially weak in the analysis of the economic forces bearing on agriculture.

This is not to say, of course, that *English Farming* was an entirely bad book. There are long passages in it which even today can be read with pleasure and profit—his discussions of the enclosure movement and of the decline of owner-occupiers, for example, are still useful. But Ernle, while certainly not unaware of the plodding and uneven character of agricultural development, leaned towards a heroic view of the great figures of the eighteenth and nineteenth centuries. Turnip Townshend, he argued, revolutionised the condition of his estate, consisting originally only of "rush-grown marshes, or sandy wastes where a few sheep starved and 'two rabbits struggled for every blade of grass'," to such effect that in a short time he quadrupled his rents. Coke of Norfolk, said Ernle, did even better, raising his rents almost ten-fold, and as the champion of "the new system of large farms and large capital" replaced "a barbarous system of cropping" by forcing upon the notice of Norfolk farmers "the practice of drilling turnips and wheat, and the value of sainfoin, swedes, mangel-wurzel and potatoes." [2] The assumption that Norfolk farming in Townshend's time, and even as late as Coke, was in a barbarous condition is the more curious because the agricultural writers well known to Ernle, and widely quoted by him, themselves recognised that the Norfolk system was not a recent innovation. And of course even a casual reading of Defoe's *Tour* (also quoted by Ernle) brings out the fact of a developed commercial farming embracing wide-spread improvements, and impresses the reader with the vigour and activity of the early eighteenth-century countryside.

The Hammonds' book, while in some ways a more thorough and perceptive piece of work than Ernle's, had something of the same defects. In effect, the Hammonds elaborated the Marxist view of enclosure as the transformation of a settled peasantry into a landless proletariat, driven by want and class legislation to face the choice of either leaving the countryside to become the exploited tools of the factory masters, or of remaining there as the degraded, under-employed and underpaid hands of the capitalist farmers. The Hammonds, it must be said, took the trouble to research among the contemporary letter-writers and pamphleteers, the Enclosure Acts and Awards, and the Home Office "blue books." But the advantage of knowing at the outset what the conclusion of the research was likely to be, made it convenient to be selective in the choice of material. This at any rate is the conclu-

[2] *Ibid.*, pp. 174–5, 217–19.

sion of those scholars like Mr. W. E. Tate who have made a painstaking
survey of the same ground.[3] And it is borne out by the Hammonds'
failure to make use of the statistical material for the early nineteenth
century which Clapham subsequently employed to such devastating
effect, and even more by their neglect of the scholarly and detailed
work by Gonner, whose book appeared in 1911, or that of A. H.
Johnson, who wrote two years earlier.[4] There is no doubt that had they
taken these writers into account their story must have been greatly
modified.

Now it may be asked, how was it that these two celebrated but
seriously imperfect books came to establish their apparently unwar-
ranted hegemony? There is no doubt that some part of Ernle's strength
lay in the quality of his prose: he commanded a style at once distinctive,
lucid, and elegant and he had remarkable powers of description. But
more important was the fact that his was the only book which, on a
large canvas and with considerable detail, covered the whole of English
farming from the Middle Ages to his own time. It still remains so, and
the latest sixth edition, which appeared so recently as 1961, has been
supplemented by a long bibliographical introduction which seeks to
bring the text up to date with "a guide to the findings and direction
of recent scholarship." [5] A perusal of this *Introduction,* however, will
have the effect of convincing most people that it is a waste of time to
continue to read Ernle.

A book which for want of any better fills the place of a standard
work is bound to have much influence, although that of Ernle must
by now be approaching vanishing point. But one reason why the traditional idea of the Agricultural Revolution has remained so firmly
entrenched is the apparent absence of anyone willing to stand forth
as the new Ernle and able to draw up into one comprehensive volume
all the devious threads of the writing of half a century. The Hammonds'
book is in different case. Following in the footsteps of Engels, Marx,
and Thorold Rogers, the Hammonds represented the radical tradition,
and they brought to bear all their considerable eloquence to present a

[3] W. E. Tate, "Opposition to Parliamentary Enclosure in the Eighteenth
Century," *Agricultural History,* XIX (July, 1945), 137–41; "Parliamentary
Counter Petitions During Enclosures of the Eighteenth and Nineteenth Cen-
turies," *English Historical Review,* LIX (September, 1944), 392–403.

[4] E. C. K. Gonner, *Common Land and Inclosure* (London: Macmillan and
Co., 1912); Arthur Henry Johnson, *The Disappearance of the Small Landowner*
(Oxford: The Clarendon Press, 1909).

[5] Ernle, *English Farming Past and Present,* Introductions by G. E. Fussell and
O. R. McGregor.

case, which while logical and well argued, persuaded primarily through its appeal to the reader's emotions and its power to convey the conviction of its authors. Historically the case was weak, relying as it did on a limited range of sources and on a relatively small body of supporting evidence. Indeed, many of the chief contentions had no sort of support at all, and the Hammonds were not the writers to bring down their readers' temperature with the kind of sobering statistics that were the tools of Gonner and Clapham. However, the Hammonds did not write for historians but for the educated public at large; and although the historians long ago rejected much of their case, the public continued to read and be convinced.

II

The gradual accumulation of new material has now reached the stage, despite certain gaps, of making it possible to reconsider the whole question of agricultural revolution in the eighteenth and nineteenth centuries. Some of this material is indeed not so new, for it involves a recognition of the work published by Clapham in the 1920's and even a reconsideration of the writings of Gonner, Johnson, and others who were contemporary with Ernle and the Hammonds. The "new" lines of thought can be said to have resulted mainly from two fields of research, one of which consists of a much more thorough and comprehensive investigation of the old sources known to Ernle, the Hammonds, and their contemporaries. The other, a new field—or at least little exploited before the last twenty-five years—consists mainly of the investigation of estate records, particularly rentals, accounts, surveys, and estate correspondence, the testamentary inventories left by farmers and cottagers, and (mainly for the nineteenth century) farmers' diaries, autobiographies, and farm accounts. In the space of an essay we cannot do more, of course, than look very briefly at this very large volume of material, but an attempt to summarise the main conclusions which have emerged from it may prove a useful undertaking. In order to achieve some sort of system in presentation we shall group the material around three main themes: the general background to agricultural development, the changes in farming methods (including those of open-field farming), and of course that subject of perennial fascination and controversy—enclosure.

The general background to agricultural development from the later seventeenth to the later nineteenth centuries has been illuminated from two directions. From one of these the historians' searchlight has been turned on the structure of landownership and the effects of this structure on agricultural development. In the first of a series of well-known essays, Professor Habakkuk showed that the late seventeenth and early eighteenth centuries saw the growth in the English countryside of large accumulations of property in the hands of great landlords, accumulations created mainly at the expense of smaller owners, the lesser gentry, and owner-occupiers. A number of the small estates were bought up also by newcomers such as retired merchants and lawyers, city and professional men.[6] In his subsequent essays Professor Habakkuk has elaborated on some of the aspects of this change, particularly the importance of the strict marriage settlement and the easier conditions for borrowing on mortgage. These developments enabled the great owners to keep their empires intact, by mitigating the risks necessarily attached to the propensity of great landlords to live beyond their incomes, and by guarding against the eventual appearance in the succession of a spendthrift, rake, or imbecile—something which happened in the best of blue-blooded families.[7]

The growth and consolidation of large estates in the eighteenth and nineteenth centuries had important implications for agricultural progress. The development helps to explain the prominence of certain large owners in the propagation of improved farming—notably Coke of Norfolk, the Dukes of Bedford, the Egremonts, Rockingham, and others—although there is now a tendency to think that the role of great owners in this respect has been exaggerated and that the farming country gentlemen, the better owner-occupiers, and large tenant-farmers formed the real spearhead of technical advance. But at least it is certain that landlords' capital was vital in providing a favourable environment for agricultural progress, the right conditions in which farmers of substance and enterprise could succeed; and these conditions included the creation of enclosed and compact farms, with adequate and suitably sited buildings, with soil kept in good condition by drainage, marling, manuring, and other means, by the commutation of tithes and a low burden of

[6] H. J. Habakkuk, "English Landownership, 1680–1740," *Economic History Review*, X (February, 1940), 2–18.

[7] H. J. Habakkuk, "Marriage Settlements in the Eighteenth Century," *Transactions of the Royal Historical Society*, XXXII (London, 1950), 15–30; "The English Land Market in the Eighteenth Century," in *Britain and the Netherlands*, eds. J. S. Bromley and E. H. Kossman (London: Chatto & Windus, 1960). See also G. E. Mingay, *English Landed Society in the Eighteenth Century* (London: Routledge and Kegan Paul, 1963), chaps. 1–4, 7, 8.

poor rates, by a moderate level of rents, and possibly—but not of necessary importance—by the provision of long leases.[8] It would be absurd to suggest that all large owners provided all these conditions, and even more absurd to suppose that they could all be provided at once. Agricultural improvement was a work of time, and its pace was limited to some extent by the availability of the necessary technical knowledge (for example, of cheap methods of under-drainage, not developed until the 1840's), as well as by the landowners' ability and willingness to spare income for investment. But the huge expenditures on enclosure in the eighteenth and early nineteenth centuries—which must have involved landlords in an investment of something over £10 million— and on drainage and buildings later in the nineteenth century, approaching £20 million, give some indication of the volume of landlords' rents that went back into improvement of the land. It should not be overlooked that the capital—and enterprise—of the landlords did much to stimulate the local economy, by the improvement of roads and the building of canals and railways, by exploiting minerals and establishing ironworks, and by developing manufactories of metal goods such as nails and agricultural implements, quarries, lime-kilns, brick-kilns, and similar projects. The general lines of this aspect of English landownership have been traced by Professor Habakkuk, by two general surveys presented before the First International Conference of Economic History, in 1960, and in other writings.[9]

[8] The provision of long leases was related partly to the size and value of the farms and partly to regional practice. Leases did not necessarily include detailed clauses laying down the farming practice to be followed, and where they did it is difficult to tell how far they were followed by the tenants. In any case, leases went much out of fashion in the nineteenth century with the severe price fluctuations and periods of depression. Many farmers wanted freedom to vary their farming as prices and other circumstances changed, and the lack of leases did not usually mean lack of security. Good landlords had a reputation for keeping their tenants, and many families carried on for generations on annual tenancies. The growth of a customary tenant right of compensation for unexhausted improvements also worked in this direction.

[9] H. J. Habakkuk, "Economic Functions of English Landowners in the Eighteenth Century," *Explorations in Entrepreneurial History,* VI (December, 1953), 92–102; G. E. Mingay, "The Large Estate in Eighteenth-Century England," and F. M. L. Thompson, "English Great Estates in the Nineteenth Century," First International Conference of Economic History, Stockholm, 1960, *Contributions* (The Hague: Mouton & Co., 1960), pp. 367–83; 385–97. See also Mingay, *English Landed Society,* chaps. 7, 8; David Spring, "The English Landed Estate in the Age of Coal and Iron, 1830–1880," *Journal of Economic History,* XI (Winter, 1951), 3–24; F. M. L. Thompson, "English Landownership: the Ailesbury Trust, 1832–56," *Economic History Review,* XI (August, 1958), 121–133; F. M. L. Thompson, "The End of a Great Estate," *Economic History*

The gathering of land into few hands also has obvious implications for the development of larger farming units and the decline of the mystical rustic—the "yeoman." Professor Habakkuk agrees with earlier writers like Davies and Johnson that the yeoman, or as the term is usually and more precisely understood, the small owner-occupier, was largely bought out in the period of active building up of great estates in the later seventeenth and early eighteenth centuries. It seems certain on the basis of the land tax assessments that the subsequent period of prosperous farming conditions enabled the surviving owner-occupiers to hold their own and even to multiply, until the big fall in prices of the 1820's. Then a further period of slow decline set in, until by the end of the nineteenth century small owner-cultivators had only about 12 per cent of the farm acreage.[10] On the whole it seems that the level of prices and the prosperity of farming had more impact on owner-occupiers than had enclosure.

Large estates, of course, had no necessary connection with large farms. In fact, it happened that many large estates had the major part of their land in undeveloped farming areas, and predominantly in small units. But the accumulation of land in the hands of large owners often encouraged consolidation, if only as a preliminary to enclosure, although again this was a slow process. It has been suggested by the present writer that the growth of larger farm units was a continuing secular process, which was under way long before the eighteenth century and did not stop with the fading out of enclosure in the nineteenth century. It was the result of a variety of influences—technical advantages of larger farms, landlords' preference for substantial tenants who could farm well and who gave less trouble in management, and the greater viability of large farmers in periods of depression. Enclosure encouraged and accelerated the process but it is clear that the engrossing of farms went on quite independently of enclosure. Indeed there is evidence to

Review, VIII (August, 1955), 36–52; David Spring, "The Earls of Durham and the Great Northern Coalfield, 1830–1880," Canadian Historical Review, XXXIII (September, 1952), 237–53; "A Great Agricultural Estate: Netherby under Sir James Graham, 1820–1845," Agricultural History, XXIX (April, 1955), 73–81.

[10] In 1800 they owned about a fifth of the cultivated acreage. See Habakkuk, "English Landownership, 1680–1740"; Johnson, Disappearance of the Small Landowner; E. Davies, "The Small Landowner, 1780–1832, in the Light of Land Tax Assessments," Economic History Review, I (January, 1927), 87–113; H. G. Hunt, "Landownership and Enclosure, 1750–1830," Economic History Review, XI (April, 1959), 497–505; John H. Clapham, Economic History of Modern Britain (3 vols., Cambridge: The University Press, 1926–38), Vol. I, p. 105.

suggest that farms grew in size more rapidly in the early eighteenth century when enclosure was limited but times were difficult, than in the later eighteenth century when enclosure went on apace but prices were rising.[11] In any event, only those who like Cobbett refused to believe official statistics could hold that small farmers disappeared in the eighteenth century, for the figures show that in 1831 nearly a half of all farmers were small.[12]

The movements of prices not only influenced the survival of owner-occupiers and small farmers but affected land use and the whole course of agricultural change. The changes in the general levels of prices meant a periodical movement from prosperity into depression and back again, with consequent influences on activity in enclosure and other agricultural investment; and in addition, differential changes in the prices of the various agricultural products determined in the long run the relative profitability of grass and arable, and hence changes in land use. Ernle and other writers of his time were aware of the general course of prices and their significance, but they failed to follow through the implications for farmers of changing market conditions. Similarly, the consequences for agricultural specialisation of the growth of towns and the increasing demand of urban populations for meat, milk, dairy produce, vegetables, fruit, and poultry were not fully considered; and neither was the impact of industrial growth on the demand for secondary products like wool, hides, tallow, and timber. There was among the writers before Clapham the same tendency towards an excessive concern with wheat, and with arable farming in general, which characterised the contemporary pamphleteers and Corn Law debates; although, as Caird pointed out, by the middle-nineteenth century the area under grass and the annual value of pasture products were approaching equality with the area and annual value of arable farming. In recent years this historical imbalance has been redressed, and much of current writing on the eighteenth and nineteenth centuries (as for earlier periods) has centered around agricultural price movements and effects on agricultural production in general, and indeed on their wider implications for the economy at large.[13]

[11] G. E. Mingay, "The Size of Farms in the Eighteenth Century," *Economic History Review*, XIV (April, 1962), 469–88.

[12] Jonathan David Chambers, *The Workshop of the World* (London: Oxford University Press, 1960), p. 75; Clapham, *op. cit.*, Vol. I, pp. 450–1, Vol. II, pp. 263–4.

[13] See A. H. John, "The Course of Agricultural Change," in *Studies in the Industrial Revolution*, ed. Leslie S. Pressnell (London: University of London,

III

Just as the investigations of eighteenth-century estate records and prices have tended to direct more attention to the earlier part of that century, so similarly have the studies concerned with farming methods shifted the focus back in time. The system of alternate husbandry—that is, the celebrated Norfolk system of alternating roots and clover with corn crops—which is now recognised, had developed long before the days of those bucolic Norfolk gentlemen, Townshend and Coke. On the neighbouring estates of the Walpole family, for example, alternate husbandry has been traced back to 1673. The basic features of Norfolk farming, the large farms, long leases, the four-course rotation, and the treatment of the soil with marl, were all well-established long before Coke was born.[14] Moreover, the practice of alternate husbandry, or some local version of it, was not confined to Norfolk or even eastern England. Turnips and clover came over from the Low Countries in the seventeenth century, if not earlier, and large areas of English farmland were influenced by the intensive methods of the Netherlands.[15] Wherever light or freely draining soils of sand or light loams were present, legumes, roots, and artificial grasses made headway, even in open-field areas.[16] On the chalk and limestone uplands, too, the early

---

Athlone Press, 1960); "Aspects of English Economic Growth in the First Half of the Eighteenth Century," *Economica* (May, 1961), 180–3; G. E. Mingay, "The Agricultural Depression, 1730–1750," *Economic History Review,* VIII (April, 1956), 323–38; T. W. Fletcher, "The Great Depression of English Agriculture, 1870–1896," *Economic History Review,* XIII (April, 1961), 417–432; W. Ashworth, *An Economic History of England: 1870–1939* (London: Methuen, 1960), chap. 3.

[14] R. A. C. Parker, "Coke of Norfolk and the Agricultural Revolution," *Economic History Review,* VIII (December, 1955), 156–66; J. H. Plumb, "Sir Robert Walpole and Norfolk Husbandry," *Economic History Review,* V. No. 1 (1952), 86–89; G. E. Fussell, Introduction to Ernle, *English Farming Past and Present,* pp. lxvi–lxxi. The importance of Coke lies mainly in his improvements of the system, his advances in the breeds of sheep and cattle kept in Norfolk, his encouragement of irrigation, under-drainage, and new manures, and the demonstration effect of his "sheep-shearings," or annual shows.

[15] G. E. Fussell, "Low Countries' Influence on English Farming," English *Historical Review,* LXXIV (October, 1959), 611–22; B. H. Slicher van Bath, "The Rise of Intensive Husbandry in the Low Countries," in *Britain and the Netherlands,* eds. J. S. Bromley and E. H. Kossman; E. Kerridge, "Turnip Husbandry in High Suffolk," *Economic History Review,* VIII (April, 1956), 390–92.

[16] M. A. Havinden, "Agricultural Progress in Open-Field Oxfordshire," *Agricultural History Review,* IX, Part 2 (1961), 75.

introduction of fodder crops into the rotations made it possible to reduce the formerly indispensable flocks of the ancient sheep-and-corn husbandry, and thus to plough up downland for crops.[17]

Alternate husbandry had thus become widespread even in the seventeenth century. Its failure to penetrate much of the Midlands and western districts, however, sprang not so much from the obtuse conservatism of the farmers, as earlier writers supposed, but because the successful growing of roots was possible only on light land and was not adaptable to the wet, cold clays. On the more amenable clay soils of the Midlands, however, fallowing was abolished by the introduction of ley-farming or convertible husbandry; that is, the periodical alternation of white crops with legumes or artificial grasses (and sometimes roots), each field being cropped for three or four years in succession, and then laid down to sainfoin or rye-grass for a similar period before being cropped again.[18] Ley-farming was far from being an eighteenth-century innovation, and was already in practice in the sixteenth century. The really evil clays—the cold, wet kind which Arthur Young advised "every friend of mine to have nothing to do with"—remained throughout the eighteenth and at least part of the nineteenth century very largely unimproved and unimprovable. For lack of adequate drainage the two corn crops and fallow continued on them long after enclosure. In the southwest of England, lastly, where grass grows readily in the winter months and the shortage of fodder was not a serious problem, small areas of turnips were sufficient, and farmers were sensibly loth to incur the heavy labour costs of the full Norfolk rotation.[19]

Progress in arable farming was thus a matter of adapting the invaluable turnip, clover, sainfoin, or rye grass to local conditions of soil and climate. Farmers were not merely stupid in failing to take over the Norfolk system, lock, stock, and barrel. Indeed, there became evident in the course of the nineteenth century a retreat from the classical four-course rotation, when the rising incidence of "finger and toe" disease in turnips and of clover-sick soil which refused to grow red clover properly, provided clear warning signs. Moreover, many farmers varied their rotations endlessly, not only in order to avoid these

[17] E. L. Jones, "Eighteenth-Century Changes in Hampshire Chalkland Farming," *Agricultural History Review*, VIII, Part 1 (1960), 5–19; R. Molland, "Agriculture c.1793–c.1870," Wiltshire *V.C.H.* IV (ed. E. Critall, 1959), 70–1.

[18] For a contemporary description see W. Marshall, *Rural Economy of Midland Counties* (1790), Vol. I, pp. 184–7.

[19] E. L. Jones, "English Farming Before and During the Nineteenth Century," *Economic History Review*, XV (August, 1962), 146.

problems, but also to take advantage of fluctuations in market conditions. The East Lothians of Scotland, with its highly flexible system, displaced Norfolk as the home of the best arable farming, and the failure of the general level of grain prices to rise substantially after the 1820's, brought about over the years another subtle change of emphasis: the growing of grain crops purely for fodder purposes, the end-product of much arable farming now being stall-fed bullocks.[20]

To complete this brief survey of developments in arable farming we should note in passing that Jethro Tull's importance has now shrunk very considerably. He was not perhaps such a crank as some writers have supposed, for he recognised that his own pet system of monoculture without manures or fallows was not applicable to all soils, and was particularly unsuitable for "wet clayey land. . . . Many, it is like," he said, "will think, this repetition of wheat crops rather a curiosity than profitable, and in some circumstances it may be so." Furthermore, there was real merit in his advocacy of sowing in drills and systematic hoeing to produce a fine tilth and to destroy weeds These ideas, however, were not new, and even Tull's design for a horse-drawn drill had been anticipated by Worlidge, who suggested a practical machine some sixty years earlier. And it seems clear that while recognizing the value of turnips as cattle food, Tull failed to perceive that it was alternate husbandry, and not the intensive pulverisation of the soil, which was the real answer to bare fallows and shortage of manure.[21]

One important consequence of the wider use of roots and artificial grasses was the increased supply of livestock. There is no doubt that the market for cattle and sheep was growing throughout the eighteenth and nineteenth centuries, and that this expanding demand lay behind the attempts to improve livestock husbandry. In his valuable books on the subject, Trow-Smith has collected for us the existing information about the earlier attempts to improve the old kinds of livestock. The principle of selective breeding had been known and put into practice for generations before Robert Bakewell appeared on the scene, and by the early eighteenth century there existed a number of well-known herds and flocks of high-quality animals. Bakewell did not begin from nothing with totally unimproved beasts, as is sometimes assumed. His

[20] *Ibid.*, p. 147; Molland, "Agriculture c. 1793–c. 1870," pp. 74–5.

[21] E. R. Wicker, "A Note on Jethro Tull: Innovator or Crank?" *Agricultural History*, XXXI (January, 1957), 47–8; T. H. Marshall, "Jethro Tull and the 'New Husbandry' of the Eighteenth Century," *Economic History Review*, II (January, 1929), 41–60; G. E. Fussell, *The Farmers' Tools*, 1500–1900 (London: Andrew Melrose, 1952), pp. 93–102.

place in agricultural history rests therefore not on the introduction of selective breeding, but rather on his successful exploitation of the advantages to be gained by breeding in and in, using only the best animals he could find for his purpose of fixing their desirable qualities in a new breed, on the lines of the highly-bred racehorses produced for the eighteenth-century aristocracy. Earlier breeders had not been able to do this, because they had not had the foresight, patience and resources to breed exclusively from the finest animals, as Bakewell did. Even Bakewell's success, however, was a limited one, for his longhorn cattle were soon destined to give way before the Collings brothers' improved shorthorns, while the flesh of his more long-lived New Leicesters was so fat that it was described as unsuitable "for genteel tables," or more explicitly as "coal-heavers' mutton." [22]

The creation of new breeds that gave general satisfaction was essentially a long process, and the ousting of the old native varieties, or rather, as in many cases, their improvement by crossing with the newer varieties, took even longer. It was well into the nineteenth century before the recognition of the importance of quality in livestock spread from the progressive few to the general run of farmers.[23]

The lesser branches of farming, such as the large and important dairying industry (with which was connected much of the production of pork, hams, and bacon), hops, fruit, market-gardening, and poultry, we must pass over, as also the lesser technical advances in such matters as water-meadows, marling, and manures. Much remains to be added to the work already produced on these subjects, but we can say at this stage that evidently they were all of considerable importance at the beginning of the eighteenth century, when English farming was already diversified and progressive. Of implements and machinery the story is different, for apart from improvements in the design of ploughs and the supplementing of the two-wheel carts by four-wheel wagons, there were few important advances that were widely adopted before the late eighteenth century. Then the developments of the Industrial Revolution eventually brought about the replacement of implements

[22] Robert Trow-Smith, *A History of British Livestock Husbandry to 1700* (London: Routledge and K. Paul, 1957); *A History of British Livestock Husbandry, 1700–1900* (London: Routledge and K. Paul, 1959), pp. 26–9, 36, 56–64.

[23] *Ibid.*, and G. E. Fussell, "The Size of English Cattle in the Eighteenth Century," *Agricultural History*, III (October, 1929), 160–181: "Eighteenth Century Estimates of English Sheep and Wool Production," *Agricultural History*, IV (October, 1930), 131–51; and "Animal Husbandry in Eighteenth Century England," *Agricultural History*, XI (April, 1937), 96–116.

of local design, constructed of wood, stone, or wrought iron, by the standardised factory product made of cast iron. It was about the 1780's that machines began to become important for lightening some of the laborious tasks of the farm, and the earliest ones included threshing machines, chaff cutters, root slicers and crushers. Many of these were first worked by hand or by horses, but eventually they were adapted to steam. However, the advance of the machines was slow, partly because many farmers were too small and too poor to buy them, partly because of the diversified output and varied growing conditions of English farming—the early American reapers, for instance, often failed in England—and partly because labour was plentiful and cheap. Only from about the 1850's did machinery become commonplace (although steam power was still highly exceptional), and only from that period could it be said to play a very significant part in agricultural output. It was about that time, too, that the invention of cheap methods of producing pipes and tiles made it possible to undertake large-scale under-drainage, the most important and most capital-absorbing of the productive improvements of the nineteenth century, comparable in these respects with the enclosure movement which was just drawing to a close.[24]

The marketing of agricultural produce remains one of the least explored areas of modern agricultural history. For much of our knowledge we are still obliged to Daniel Defoe, whose *Tour of England and Wales,* while tending perhaps to over-emphasize the importance of the London market, evokes a comprehensive picture of a bustling, highly commercialised agriculture, catering considerably for distant markets— a picture that we cannot ignore.[25] Fussell has used this and other sources to give us a valuable but inevitably vague account of eighteenth-century traffic in farm produce and of trade routes; and Mathias has thrown useful light on the important market offered by the brewing and distilling industries.[26] The rest is silence.

However, it is possible to say that we know much more about

---

[24] *History of Technology,* eds. Charles Singer, et al. (5 vols., New York: Oxford University Press, 1956–58), Vol. IV, chaps. 1, 2; Fussell, *The Farmers' Tools;* Clapham, *Economic History of Modern Britain,* Vol. I, pp. 458–62, Vol. II, pp. 267–73.

[25] D. Defoe, *A Tour Through England and Wales* (Everyman's edition; London: J. M. Dent & Sons, 1928).

[26] G. E. Fussell and C. Goodman, "The Eighteenth-Century Traffic in Livestock," *Economic History,* III (February, 1936), 214–36; "Traffic in Farm Produce in Eighteenth-Century England," *Agricultural History,* XII (October, 1938), 355–68; P. Mathias, "Agriculture and the Brewing and Distilling Industries in the Eighteenth Century," *Economic History Review,* V, No. 2 (1952), 249–57.

open-field farming than we did even a dozen years ago. Young, of course, exaggerated the backwardness of the "goths and vandals" of open-field farmers, as he did so much else; but, as Professor Tawney once commented, it is now well understood that the open fields were not "a miracle of squalid petrifaction," nor their cultivators "the slaves of organized torpor." Of course, there were plenty of villages with only two fields, one of which was always bare-fallowed, with inconveniently dispersed and highly-fragmented holdings, and with over-stocked commons that periodically saw the livestock decimated by epidemic disease. But by the eighteenth century or earlier, many open-field villages had gradually overcome or mitigated these defects. In some areas the number of fields was increased to three, four, or even more, in order to diversify the rotations and reduce the area of fallow. Often there was no longer a rigid succession of crops, and the introduction of clover, sainfoin, and turnips into the rotations, or as leys, largely obviated fallowing and made it possible to support a larger number of beasts. The area under white crops consequently declined but there was now more manure to keep the arable in better heart.[27] Thus the "open-field system" was adapted to reap the advantages of alternate husbandry, and the age-old problem of inadequacy of winter fodder was at least partially solved. Dr. Hoskins found evidence that convertible husbandry in the open fields (i.e. leys) goes "well back into the sixteenth century, and probably earlier than that."[28] The sources of fodder were augmented by always keeping one of the fields in grass (or preferably in clover or sainfoin, which were far more nutritious), by leaving leys in the open fields, and furthermore by establishing water-meadows and by permanently enclosing large pieces of the open fields for additional stocking or dairying closes. The eventual enclosure of the open-field leys and the creation of closes for permanent pasture were factors in the piecemeal process by which the open-field area of many "unenclosed" villages was reduced to quite a small proportion of the total cultivated land. At the same time there was often a good deal of

[27] Havinden, "Agricultural Progress in Open-Field Oxfordshire," pp. 75–82.

[28] William G. Hoskins, "The Leicestershire Farmer in the Seventeenth Century," *Agricultural History*, XXV (January, 1951), 14–17, 20; also his *The Midland Peasant* (London: Macmillan, 1957), pp. 162–4; 235–6. Dr. Hoskins' examination of testamentary inventories has thrown light not only on the development of open-field farming but also on housing conditions and the distribution of wealth in rural communities. For further discussions see E. M. Gardner, "East Sussex Inventories," *Sussex Notes and Queries*, XV (1959); G. H. Kenyon, "Kirdford Inventories, 1611–1776," *Sussex Archaeological Collections*, XCIII (1955); Francis W. Steer, *Farm and Cottage Inventories of Mid-Essex, 1635–1749* (Chelmsford: Essex County Council, 1950).

consolidation and engrossing, and open-field farms grew larger, more compact and easier to work.

IV

Open-field farming thus developed towards a more flexible and efficient husbandry employing turnips, legumes, and artificial grasses on increasingly larger and more compact farms, which often included a fair proportion of enclosed permanent pasture or ley ground. It follows, of course, that many enclosures merely speeded up and completed this process, and the view that all enclosures brought about a transformation of the farming system and represented the sudden overthrow of a traditional and completely obsolete structure is untenable. This is extremely important because it makes clear the hazards of generalising about a process, the character and effects of which were in fact highly diverse. Each village had its own peculiar features in relation to soil and topography, markets and communications, the area of commons and waste and the size of the remaining open fields, the existing system of cultivation, whether developed or still backward, and the structure of landownership and farm sizes, to mention only the more obvious variables, and each of these had some influence on the course taken by enclosure.

Insofar as we may risk generalisation, we can say that the great weight of modern evidence leads us to believe that the earlier writers like the Hammonds grossly exaggerated the influence of enclosure and ascribed to it consequences that derived more from price movements, industrialisation, population growth, and other factors. The clearest reason for reconsidering the importance of enclosure is that the evils popularly thought to have been its peculiar results such as rural unemployment and poverty, the engrossing of farms, decline of small owners and large rent increases, were very often found equally in villages quite untouched by the enclosures of the eighteenth and nineteenth centuries. Indeed, pauperism was more marked in counties like Kent and Sussex, where enclosure was negligible, than in some other areas which were exposed to the full flood of the movement, and in the last labourers' revolt of 1830 it is clear that enclosures were not an important factor.[29]

[29] Compare Gonner's table of expenditure on poor relief (*Common Land and Inclosure*, p. 448) with the Hammonds' account of the revolt, in *The Village Labourer*, p. 105, and chaps. 11, 12.

On the purely agricultural effects we can say with assurance that enclosure did not always have an immediate or very drastic effect on the system of cultivation. This was partly because much progress had been made already in developing the open-field husbandry, and partly because some heavy soils could not depart from the traditional two crops and fallow until cheap under-drainage was available. In general, enclosure naturally had the effect of accelerating the spread of improved farming and helped to achieve greater efficiency by creating compact farms in individual occupation, but perhaps the expansion of the cultivated acreage by the intake of commons and wastes was at least as important for the increase of total output. We have seen already that there was a secular trend towards larger farms and the displacement of owner-occupiers, which proceeded independently of enclosure although it may have been accelerated by it.[30] To suppose a sudden wholesale engrossing of farms as the result of enclosure is absurd in view of the nineteenth-century figures of farm sizes; and indeed such a supposition involves a further absurdity, for it assumes that lurking somewhere in the hedgerows were large numbers of capitalist farmers, all boasting capitals of £1,000 or more, and impatiently waiting for the enclosure commissioners to do their work that they might step in and gobble up the peasant holdings. Furthermore, the customary fairness of the enclosure commissioners, the low average levels of enclosure costs, and the wide possibilities of borrowing which existed in the eighteenth-century countryside are all recently established considerations which collectively must throw great doubt on the supposed grounds for the collapse of the "yeomen." [31] Of course, there were undoubtedly *some* enclosures which brought about rapid changes in the farming system, the structure of ownership, the size of farms, and in employment. The extent of these changes was largely determined by local or regional circumstances, particularly those of soil, availability of waste lands, and the most profitable use of the land. But it seems unlikely that the changes unfavourable to the small peasantry which were the results of enclosure in some areas were the typical consequences of enclosure in general.

The effects of enclosure on the labouring population, however, are

[30] See Mingay, "Size of Farms," Habakkuk, "English Landownership," and further references in fn. 10.

[31] W. E. Tate, "Opposition to Parliamentary Enclosure," "Parliamentary Counter Petitions," and "The Cost of Parliamentary Enclosure in England (with special reference to Oxfordshire)," *Economic History Review*, V, No. 2 (1952), 258–65.

perhaps more disputable. On the side of loss we have the enclosure of commons and the possibility that increased areas of permanent pasture caused local unemployment. But between 1760 and 1815, when the bulk of Parliamentary enclosures were carried out, market considerations make it likely that much more of the newly enclosed land went under the plough than down to grass. And Clapham pointed out a generation ago the fallacy in thinking that every labourer lost a cow, or indeed lost anything at all of much value when the commons were enclosed. It is even more fallacious to visualise the creation of an agricultural proletariat as dating from the Enclosure Acts, for even in 1690, as Clapham again noted, there were already nearly two landless labourers to every occupier, and in 1831 still only a proportion of two and a half to one.[32] Finally, in one of the most important contributions of recent years, J. D. Chambers has examined the connections between rural employment, migration, enclosure, and population growth. His main conclusions are that enclosure greatly increased employment by expanding the area under cultivation and by extending the growing of labour-absorbing crops like turnips and the legumes; the total numbers employed in farming were rising, but it was the more rapid growth of population which created the surplus of labour from which the industrial labour force was drawn.[33]

The effect of all this new work on enclosure compels us to re-assess its significance in modern agricultural history. The early twentieth-century generation of historians over-estimated its importance, first because both before and since Marx it had loomed large in the story of agricultural change; secondly, because it provided a ready-made explanation of changes that were not otherwise easily explicable; and lastly, perhaps, because the readily accessible material in Enclosure Acts and Awards made it an easy and obvious subject to study. It must be conceded that the far more complex picture which we now have lacks the unity of the old one, as it lacks also its appeal of monolithic simiplicity; but the modern explanation bears much more the appearance of truth and historical probability. It is of course in the nature of history that the evidence produced by more detailed investigation of a wider range of sources will tend eventually to overthrow the more

[32] Clapham, *Economic History of Modern Britain*, Vol. I, pp. 113–21.
[33] J. D. Chambers, "Enclosure and Labour Supply in the Industrial Revolution," *Economic History Review*, V, No. 3 (1953), 322–4. This supplements the point made by Redford in his *Labour Migration in England* (1926), pp. 59–60, that the migration of labour from the countryside into the towns was responsive more to the state of industrial employment than to agricultural conditions.

conjectural assessments of an earlier generation. Indeed, in view of the great volume of new evidence now in print it is remarkable that the romantic attraction of the traditional story should remain so durable. But then we have still to find our new Ernle and our new Hammonds.

V

What remains of the traditional Agricultural Revolution? Mainly, the still remarkable fact that even in 1870, when the population had grown to become some five times as large as it was in 1700, 80 per cent of the people could still be fed from home-produced food—from land cultivated by only 14 per cent of the labour force. The implications of this for industrial development and economic growth are evident and need not be laboured. This striking increase in agricultural output resulted, in brief, from greatly improved farming methods applied to a considerably increased farm acreage, the major part of the land being cultivated in fairly large units under a system of landownership and management, which despite some failings, nevertheless encouraged a heavy investment of capital and achieved a high degree of efficiency. Does this amount to "agricultural revolution"? The full development of this varied, intricate, and highly productive system of agriculture took much longer to evolve than we used to think; this is the main lesson of the new evidence. Nevertheless, if we consider the enormous magnitude of the change and the complexity of its diverse advance—rather than merely the time-period involved—we may yet come to think that "agricultural revolution" should not be relegated to the historians' lumber room of discarded terminology.

THE PLACE OF THE REVOLUTION IN THE AGRARIAN HISTORY OF FRANCE *

Georges Lefebvre

Georges Lefebvre, before his death Professor of the History of the French Revolution at the Sorbonne, was a pioneer in diverting the

* From *Annales d'histoire économique et sociale*, Vol. I, No. 4 (1929). Reprinted by permission of the editors of *Annales: Économies-Sociétés-Civilisations*. Translated by James Friguglietti.

*attention of historians away from Revolutionary Paris to the country-
side, where the peasantry, who formed about three-quarters of the
total population, lived. The selection below explains how far the Revolution went in satisfying peasant aspirations, how short it fell, and
why. The influence of long-standing agrarian conditions on the
Revolutionary land settlement is clearly brought out.*

I

There is no need to dwell on the importance of the peasant question in the history of the French Revolution. In 1789 France was an
essentially rural country, so that it is unimaginable that any transformation of society could have taken place without the peasants' making
their presence felt. The new regime could not have consolidated itself
if the peasants had shown no interest in its fate.

This being the case, what measures among all those passed by the
Revolutionary assemblies particularly affected the peasantry? Two
kinds have usually been distinguished: on the one hand, the abolition
of privileges (especially in taxes) and the suppression of the tithe
and of feudal dues, which were decided upon, at least in principle,
on the night of August 4, 1789; and, on the other, the sale of national
property. Both have attracted the attention of those historians who
have devoted themselves to the study of the economic and social history
of the Revolution. Although this work is not very far advanced, the
facts which have been learned enable us to consider some of these
questions from a fresh point of view. Until now, the history of the
Revolution has ordinarily been written from inside the Revolutionary
assemblies or administrations. The laws have been analyzed, the efforts
of the authorities to apply them have been described, and (to a far
lesser degree) the results achieved have been evaluated. But, in the
last analysis, it has always been stated that the achievements of the
Revolution completely fulfilled the peasants' wishes. Some have condemned its acts as being the most radical imaginable; others, who
approved of them, could scarcely conceive that at least a part of the
peasantry might have desired to go even further.

And yet the history of the abolition of feudal rights clearly presents
a problem. The taking of the measure was imposed on the Constituent
Assembly by the agrarian uprisings of July, 1789, for virtually all peasants were united against their seigneurs. But while the Revolutionary
bourgeoisie found no difficulty in proclaiming civil equality and sup-

pressing the tithe, they experienced great scruples where seignorial rights (which applied to private property and were also possessed by many of these same bourgeois) were concerned. The Constituent Assembly sought to escape from its dilemma by submitting this category of property to judicial review. The jurists distinguished between two types of property rights: first, such rights as mortmain,[1] which were illegally acquired and contrary to natural law, or manorial courts, which usurped the state's right to dispense justice, or *banalités*,[2] which were supposedly imposed by force; and second, manorial dues which, they declared, represented payments on the grant of a landed holding. The former were abolished without compensation, while the latter had to be redeemed. The peasants would not accept this distinction, considering manorial dues abolished along with the other rights, and either refused to redeem them or did so only with great reluctance. After the overthrow of Louis XVI in 1792 and his execution in 1793, when France was invaded by foreign powers and torn by royalist and Girondin uprisings, the Legislative Assembly and the Convention decided to do away with redemption in order to assure the support of the peasantry. Finally, by the Law of July 17, 1793, all feudal rights were completely abolished without compensation. There can be no doubt, then, that the partial measures taken by the Constituent Assembly failed to fulfill the peasants' wishes, and that it took the outright abolition of all feudal rights by the Convention to satisfy them.

With this in mind, should we not ask similar questions concerning the sale of national property? It is well known that, for financial reasons, the Constituent Assembly declared church property at the disposal of the nation and decreed that it be sold. To this store the Convention later added the estates formerly held by the Crown. The Convention also decided to alienate the property of secondary schools (the *collèges*), charitable institutions, condemned prisoners, deported priests, and, most important, the émigrés. The needs of the Treasury determined the conditions of sale: all national property was sold at auction, and this method in turn decided its distribution among the different classes of the nation. It naturally fell into the hands of the most wealthy or (to phrase it differently) the least poor. It is true that the Law of 28 Ventôse, Year IV (March 18, 1796) passed under the Directory did away with these auctions in favor of sale by individual bidding, but

[1] The right whereby the property of a peasant who had no children reverted to the seigneur. [Editor's note.]

[2] The obligatory use (and payment therefore) of an object or facility—such as a grist-mill—which by right belonged exclusively to the seigneur. [Editor's note.]

we cannot overlook the fact that the rich man and the speculator found this an opportunity to shut out the poor even more effectively. In 1793 the Montagnard Convention did indeed vote laws that sought to favor buyers of modest means and even the indigent. But although the laws had some effect the practice of sale at auction was maintained and the Convention's social policies were thereby sacrificed to necessity in order to prop up the value of the assignat.[3] In short, throughout the Revolution, national property was offered primarily to the richest, and in this respect the policy of the Convention did not differ radically from that of the Constituent Assembly. This is in contrast to what we have seen with regard to landed manorial dues.

Must we therefore conclude that the peasants were fully and unanimously satisfied with these methods of disposal? Should we consider the Montagnard laws, timid as they were, as demagogic measures intended for display purposes only, measures which the masses had not demanded and from which they did not seek to profit because they had no wish to acquire land? But if the contrary is true, why did the peasants not *compel* the Revolutionary assemblies to modify this legislation as they had already modified that covering feudal rights? There are perhaps few more important problems in the agrarian history of France.

II

For the sale of national property at auction to have satisfied all the peasants of France, there would have had to be no agrarian crisis; that is, each of them would have possessed enough land to be able to live independently. It could be said that they watched impassively while the bourgeoisie and more well-to-do members of the peasantry gobbled up national property, but this was not the case.

The truth is that, if we compare France to England and to Eastern Europe, the most striking feature that emerges is the superior status of the French peasant. Generally speaking he was free like the English peasant, and even where he was still a serf or subject to mortmain, his obligations bore no comparison to those of the German *Unterthan* or the Eastern serf. *Gesinde Dienst,* or arbitrary forced labor, was unknown in France. Moreover, the French peasant was often a landowner (subject, of course, to the payment of manorial dues), while the great majority of English peasants were reduced to the condition

[3] Paper money backed by the value of the national properties. [Editor's note.]

of simple day laborers, and those of Eastern Europe who worked a holding generally held it on a rather precarious basis. What was the extent of peasant-held property in France? It varied greatly from one region to another, even those bordering on each other, and often from village to village. It was considerable in certain parts of Flanders, Alsace, and Aquitaine, very limited in regions of marsh, wood, and heath, and extremely small around Versailles. Until local variations are known, all that can be said for certain is that the proportion ranged from 30 to 40 per cent.

But this is still not all, for when we describe France simply as a country of small landowners, we overlook the most striking feature of its rural physiognomy, that characteristic which may indeed have silently exerted the greatest influence. In England the aristocracy, having brought together large farms through enclosure, rented them to a small number of farmers who were usually well-to-do and educated. In eastern Germany the *Gutsheer* himself exploited his vast estates by means of compulsory labor owed him by his peasants. In France, on the contrary, priest, noble, and bourgeois almost never farmed their property, which was very fragmented, but rented it out in estates of modest size, and even in small plots. Virtually all the property of the curés, parishes, and the poor fell into the last category. Thus a considerable number of French peasants rented their farms. A few were large farmers, with small sharecroppers comprising the majority, but even many day laborers were able to secure a piece of meadow-land or garden. Not all these tenants were landowners as well. Large farmers often owned nothing, though many small proprietors found a way to round out their property by adding slivers held on lease.

This meant that almost all the cultivable land in France was already exploited directly by the peasants, who operated on their own initiative and at their own risk. So, once again, the condition of the peasantry, varying widely as it did from one region to another depending on how much land the aristocracy and bourgeoisie owned, also varied in extent from one family to another. The disunion of the peasant mass was already far advanced. Against their common enemy, the seigneur, there was considerable unity, but the individual interests of large farmer, sharecropper, and day laborer were vastly different. This situation would have been far more marked if the family community, still very common, had not remained undivided. This was not (as has been frequently repeated) because of compulsory inheritance laws—peasant property was not subject to primogeniture, and the

freedom to make wills was still very limited. It was due rather to
general economic conditions which did not favor the awakening of
individualism among the humble.

III

In any case, a careful examination still reveals that there was indeed an agrarian crisis. First, simply to repeat that France was a
country of small landowners does not mean that every peasant was one.
The proportion of heads of families who owned neither land nor even
a cottage was quite variable, but the regions where it was low are the
exception. In the coastal plains of Flanders, 75 per cent of heads of
families owned no property, in some villages around Versailles, 70
per cent, and in lower Normandy, 30 to 40 per cent. Renting of land
diminished these figures greatly in Flanders, and to a far lesser degree
in lower Normandy, but it never reduced them to zero. Thus, there
existed in France, as in England, a genuine agricultural proletariat.
True, it was very unevenly distributed, yet each of its members ar-
dently desired to acquire or rent a piece of land, if only a wretched
cottage with a garden. In the eighteenth century there were constant
complaints about usurpation committed against the common lands,
principally on the edge of the forest, by poor souls seeking something
to call their own.

Secondly, the vast majority of small peasants did not hold enough
land to live independently. South of the River Lys in the future Nord
Department, three-quarters of those who worked the soil owned less
than a hectare. This is why the usurpation of common lands cannot
be attributed exclusively to the indigent and explains, too, why the
cahiers called for the sale of crown land and occasionally that of the
clergy. To the produce from their farms, the peasants were forced to
add whatever other resources they could, earning extra income from
the more well-to-do cultivators, especially in the harvest and grape-
gathering seasons or by practicing a trade, most often in the employ of
a merchant in a nearby town. But not all succeeded in making both
ends meet, and those who failed had to resort to begging. In bad years
the number of beggars could speedily assume dangerous proportions.

This situation was aggravated because in the last years of the old
regime the population of France was increasing fairly rapidly and the
price of goods rose continually.

IV

The crisis had obvious demographic causes and, in this respect, it was irremediable in itself. The only solutions left would have been to impel the peasants into industry or to advise them to emigrate. But the crisis also had economic and social causes, for which there could be two remedies—either to improve agriculture so that the farmer could live off an increasingly small plot, or to give land to those peasants who lacked it by dividing large farms or expropriating it from landowners who did not work their own soil.

In eighteenth-century France the progress of agriculture ran counter not only to the routine of the illiterate peasant, but also to the interests of the rural masses, which have usually been too lightly dismissed. Except in Flanders where fallowing had virtually disappeared, arable land was generally divided into three parts: one-third was sown in wheat, a second reserved for spring grain, and the third remained uncultivated. After the harvest was gathered, both fallow and cultivated fields became common land subject to common pasture, where all peasants might send their cattle. This was also the case with meadow-land after the second mowing and, quite often, even after the first. It must be added that a great many plots remained fallow for far more than one year. In western France and the mountains the soil was cultivated only at very long intervals. Finally, in numerous regions, common land, heath, waste, marsh, and forest were quite extensive, and the customary rights of usage in private or crown woodlands—pasturage and the cutting of firewood or building timber—disappeared only slowly and with difficulty. Nor should we forget the rights to glean and to pull up the stubble, which was left high by the use of sickles.

Thus a landowner was far from exercising the full rights over his property expounded under Roman law. Even if, as in Alsace and eastern and northern France, custom was not binding upon him, respect for the three-field system of the village community and for common pasture compelled him in fact to bow before the practice of those proprietors whose lands bordered his own. In the thinking of the rural classes, even enclosure did not always permit one individual to shut out the cattle of others. For this reason, agricultural progress remained very difficult and the upgrading of pasture land and the development of artificial meadows even more so. Yet to the rural masses their collective customary rights were as sacred as any other, and (for want of legal title) based on prescription. In fact, the existence of most peasants depended on them. Those who did not farm much land or who had none at all could nevertheless raise a cow, a pig, or a few sheep, thanks to common pasture. Without this resource it would have been impossible for the peasants to live. Progress in agriculture could be achieved only at the expense of the poor.

Much the same was true of the price rise which resulted in part from free trade in grain and other commodities. The day laborer could at least afford to buy grain to feed his family, but many small land-owners, having had to sell theirs in order to pay taxes, found themselves in short supply by the end of summer, and the sharecropper was in even worse straits. Those who profited from the price rise were the large farmers, big landowners, tithe collectors, and seigneurs who collected landed dues. Thus the great majority of peasants were in favor of regulation and price controls, just as the townspeople were.

So it was in fact against peasant custom and self-interest that the monarchy directed its agricultural policy toward the end of the old regime. Concerned with ending the famines that inevitably provoked unrest, and with increasing the amount of foodstuffs on which the growth of population and, hence, the supply of tax-payers and eventual recruits for the army depended; sensitive to the economists' pleas and the example set by the English; and, finally, influenced by the great landowners who desired to increase their revenues, the monarchy pro-mulgated edicts in several provinces which authorized landowners to carry out enclosure that did away with common lands, and edicts of partition permitting seigneurs to seize one-third of the communal property in their parishes. This policy encouraged land clearing and drainage, which had the result of reducing pasturage accordingly. In-creased prices for grain and commodities were achieved through the development of roads and canals, the Treaty of Commerce of 1786 with England, and especially by allowing free movement of grain, which could even be exported as permitted by the Edict of 1787. In short, it was a policy which stirred the grower to produce for sale and profit like the English farmer or the Prussian Junker. But these efforts had only a moderate success and aroused growing anger.

For one thing, it was often difficult to carry out enclosure without redistributing property, and such a massive enterprise as redistribution was never envisaged. The monarchy would certainly have rejected it out of a fear of uprooting the peasantry, and thus of disturbing the collection of taxes and increasing the floating population. But even the seigneurs themselves seem scarcely to have given it any thought. In effect, the landed dues that constituted an essential element of their income were attached to existing holdings. It would have been impossible in practice, as well as very dangerous in all respects, to have attempted any redistribution of land encumbered with dues. Some large landowners were content with maneuvering to annex small farms into one or more large holdings within their own domains. Moreover, numerous administrators and agronomists remained in favor of small holdings for both political and economic reasons.

Another problem was that the new economy could provide profits only to large cultivators and landowners. They alone could gain from the rise in the price of commodities and from enclosure, while partition was frankly to the advantage of the seigneurs. The rural masses protested vigorously and occasionally resisted openly. More than once, local authorities took their side. The decrease in pasture land not only increased misery but also made the collection of taxes more difficult, and, by provoking a decline in stock raising, hurt the towns through increased prices for meat, milk, butter, and cheese.

In any case, the agrarian crisis could not have been solved by an increase in production which would have been slower than the growth of population. The royal administration had no such lofty ambitions either. In its view the best remedy for helping the poor peasants (other than charity) lay in the development of rural industry, which was given free rein during the last years of the old regime and which grew remarkably in certain regions like the North, Picardy, and Normandy. But even in these areas it was merely an insufficient palliative, while many others, like Limousin, by 1789 had still not begun to profit from it.

Yet the policy of the old regime was not badly conceived and could indeed have contributed to the maintenance of order and the strengthening of the authority and prestige of the monarchy. But for this, two conditions were necessary: the greatest possible number of peasants would have had to benefit from it (something that could have been achieved only by subjecting the privileged classes to taxation, and by suppressing the tithe and feudal rights, or at least by commuting these burdens into monetary dues); and the impression would have to be eradicated that the king's intervention in agrarian affairs was destined to favor the aristocracy. But since the edicts of partition had obviously been mainly to the aristocracy's advantage, it may be said that the

reforms of the old regime in fact only precipitated its fall by over-
exciting the peasantry. During the agrarian troubles that began in the
spring of 1789 and which deteriorated into a general uprising by the
end of July, the peasants did not confine their attacks to a refusal to
pay the tithe and manorial dues to the seigneurs. It is too little known
that the peasants seized the opportunity also to recover possession of
those collective rights which had been taken from them. Everywhere
they destroyed enclosures and reopened common pasture, restored the
seignorial third to community property, and invaded the forests. Everywhere, too, they halted the movement of grain and demanded fixed
prices for it, just as the urban population did. From all the evidence,
the desire of the great majority of the peasantry was to maintain the
traditional system of agriculture and customary regulations which, in
fact, limited property rights.

V

In these conditions it may be said that, for the peasant, there was
but one solution to the agrarian crisis—a law which would limit the
size of farms so as to multiply them or, at least, prevent them from
being diminished in number, and which would also distribute the
greatest possible amount of land to the peasants for farming purposes.

The old regime did not fail to take these measures into consideration. The legal division of holdings was far too alien to its agricultural
policy for it to adopt, but it asked nothing better than to increase the
number of small proprietors. By favoring land clearance, the regime
indirectly encouraged the usurpation of common lands, and more than
once we find the peasants showing that they regarded the declarations
of 1764 and 1766 as implicit authorization to take full ownership. The
edicts of partition permitted or ordered the division of the two-thirds
left to the parish. But the wishes of the peasantry went far beyond this.
The *cahiers* often demanded the sale of royal domains and occasionally
made mention of church property. The division of common land was
a far less satisfactory solution. Since such land was of greatest benefit
to those peasants who owned cattle, the poorer ones generally leaned
toward partition, but the decline in pasturage gave them good cause
to hesitate.

When the Constituent Assembly placed church property and the
royal domains on sale, the peasants in regions where this land was
extensive—notably Picardy and the area around Versailles—hoped

either to acquire it at a modest cost or that it would be distributed to them, at least in part, in return for an annual rent, on the basis (for example) of one *arpent* [1] for each household. When they saw that they were to be disappointed, their rage often exploded. In June, 1793, the Convention had to grant indigent peasants the lease of an *arpent* in order to calm those living near Versailles. In Picardy in 1791 and 1792 the peasants violently interfered with auctions so as to acquire their village lands at the assessed price. As we have seen, the Montagnards tried to calm the peasantry by partitioning lands and dividing property before placing it on sale. But, since public bidding was required, complaints continued, as the petitions of 1793 and 1794 (most of which have never been published) clearly prove. The sans-culotte administrators pointed out more than once that the conditions of sale continued to discourage the poor. These same petitions insisted with particular force on the need to divide up large farms and to regulate sharecropping, since the sale of national property involved only a very small area and often, too, left holdings intact. The peasant drive may possibly explain, for one thing, why the *Enragés* and Hébertists frequently demanded the confiscation of the property of all suspects, and why the Robespierrists (as Albert Mathiez believed) thought that, in the Ventôse decrees of 1794 which promised to distribute suspects' property to the poor, they had found the means to attach the peasants to the Montagnard revolution. It may also help explain the development of Babeuf's ideas about agrarian communism, since he was a Picard and had lived among a peasantry who, more than any other, practiced collective action in order to lay their hands on national property.

VI

But the members of the Revolutionary assemblies, whatever their other opinions and policies, remained almost unanimously hostile to the desire of the poor peasants for the maintenance of traditional agriculture and regulations, and the distribution (at least in part) of national property. Peasants were rare in their ranks, and these necessarily belonged to the well-to-do class. The other deputies undoubtedly had some contact with the countryside, but they too maintained relations with the peasant middle class. The rural code of the Constituent Assembly, which the Convention did not touch, granted the landowner

[1] Old French measure. Roughly an acre. [Editor's note.]

full rights over his property. It authorized him to carry out enclosure, thereby doing away with common pasture, and permitted him to exploit it in complete freedom, implicitly removing all legal force from the regulations of the old rural community. Like the Constituent Assembly, the Convention remained deaf to petitions demanding the division of large farms and the regulation of sharecropping. Free trade in grain and agricultural commodities became one of the principles of the new regime. The memory of the Maximum was invoked in vain. The Montagnard deputies saw price control imposed by the sans-culottes of the towns, but accepted it only reluctantly. If they later perceived that, like requisitioning, it was a useful war measure, they never considered including it among the permanent institutions of the Republic. As for national property, the assemblies never forgot that it was destined primarily to support the assignat. The Montagnards themselves maintained sales at auction, and not the slightest objection seems to have been raised to the Law of April 24, 1793, which forbade peasants to form associations to guarantee that lands would be awarded to their communes. After having granted the indigent the lease of an *arpent* of land on June 3, 1793, the Montagnard Convention in September of that year subjected these leases to sale at auction, and only at the end of the Year II, when the Thermidorians of the left felt themselves threatened by the growing reaction, did some among them protest against the monopolizing of national property by the rich. Mathiez would have us believe that, by deciding to confiscate the property of all suspects and to distribute it to the indigent, the Robespierrists precipitated their own fall, so greatly did a measure of this kind repel their colleagues. Still, the agrarian crisis would not have been resolved for all that—the thought of putting an end to it never preoccupied the Revolutionaries. In his report on the agrarian troubles around Versailles that had motivated the decree of June 3, 1793, Delacroix declared positively that the rural poor ought to turn to industry; and that to provide them with land would deprive the manufacturer and businessman of manpower.

Thus the agrarian development of France continued along the same path as in the eighteenth century. As in many other realms, the Revolution achieved promptly and energetically what the monarchy had only timidly considered almost without realizing it. Not that French agriculture was transformed, inasmuch as fallowing and common pasture persisted for a long time. But the legal obstacles that hindered individual initiative were broken. And in another respect, the Revolution, like the monarchy before it, proved rather favorable to small land-owners and small farmers, without destroying large-scale farming, since the sale of national property and the partition of common lands would necessarily increase their numbers to some degree. An economist might detect some contradiction between the two extremes of the Revolutionary policy, for small-scale farming and subdivision of agricultural land were not conducive to a rapid transformation of agriculture. But, socially, this economic contradiction was a source of harmony. The agricultural revolution could operate only at the expense of the peasant who had little or no land. Slowness alone could soften its harsher consequences. Besides, if it was longer in coming, it thus benefited a greater number.

VII

But we cannot help asking why the peasants, who acted with such vigor against the aristocracy and who, through their united resistance, eventually compelled the Revolutionary assemblies to abolish feudal rights entirely, did not remain united in order to oblige the assemblies also to reinforce regulation, maintain collective rights, and to distribute all or part of the national property to the rural classes.

First, peasant solidarity was complete only against the seigneur. As has been shown, the peasant masses were already too disunited not to be divided where other agrarian questions were involved. The large farmer could only gain by remaining master of his own holdings and selling his grain freely, and he was not displeased that national property was put up at auction, because he was rich enough to buy. Too, he exercised considerable influence in the village since he provided work, tilled the lands of peasants without farm animals, and sold grain to those who lacked it. Those peasants who were already landowners might well hesitate, depending on their circumstances. No doubt many would have gladly welcomed more democratic methods of land disposal, but being accustomed to acquiring land on an individual basis and as a result of their own personal efforts, they could not fail to seize the opportunity being offered. Once they had profited from it or even began to covet it, they became separated spiritually from the cause of the village proletariat. Henceforth, their complete adaptation to economic liberalism was merely a question of time.

Nor could there be the same solidarity between different regions, or even between village and village, in the face of the agrarian crisis, as had united them in regard to feudal rights. The question of collective rights presented itself in different forms in each part of France. The extent of church property varied in the extreme—in western and southern France little of it existed. The situation with respect to émigré property was even more complicated, for many villages had none, since not all the nobles had emigrated and those who remained were not all guillotined, as some foreigners and even a few Frenchmen often suppose. In those communes with little national property, the peasants had scant opportunity to acquire any.

In Eastern Europe, where a somewhat similar situation currently exists, at least a temporary solution to the agrarian crisis has been found, not only at the expense of property subject to mortmain or that of the enemies of the state, since all large estates have been expropriated and divided among the peasants. Likewise, the French peasants might have demanded that the Republic buy back, even with worthless assignats, the land necessary to satisfy them. That feature which we have noted as being the most striking in the agrarian makeup of France explains why they did not think of it (at least as far as we know). The lands which would have had to be expropriated and divided were already in the hands of the peasants either by reason of sharecropping or rent. These peasants were quite numerous and often very humble. True, each of them would have received a plot of his own by partition, but he would have lost a far more extensive holding, one on which he could live or which rounded out his own property. We can sense the importance of this consideration from the deep emotion that swept the countryside at the end of 1790, when there was fear lest the Constituent Assembly allow purchasers of national property to cancel leases. So the turn of events can be partly explained by the long agrarian history of France.

This said, the cause must also be related to the policy of the Revolutionary assemblies. The Constituent Assembly ordered that the different parcels of the same farm be put up for auction at intervals and that preference be given to separate bids over bids for the whole provided the former yielded the same amount to the Treasury. As has been seen, the Montagnards went further: they decreed that lands must be divided into parcels and sold separately. Both granted very long delays in payment. Furthermore, the Convention authorized the division of common lands and, in municipalities which possessed none, allowed the indigent to acquire 500 *livres'* worth of national property, payable in twenty years. Even though there is some uncertainty as to the amount of peasant income, there is no doubt that many were able to round out their property and that a considerable number became landowners. It is also certain that, with the dividing up of many farms, the number of those who rented them became more considerable. Other circumstances added weight to the laws, for many nobles and bourgeois, ruined by conditions or bankruptcy, sold their property— and the peasants benefited. So the ranks of the rural proletariat undoubtedly were thinned. There is no reason to consider the members of the Revolutionary assemblies as Machiavellians acting out of class interest, nor any need to accuse them of having behaved like cunning, greedy bourgeois who sought to divide their opponents and get the lion's share for themselves. Like many officials and agronomists of the old regime, numerous members of the Constituent Assembly sincerely believed in the need to multiply small holdings in the interest of agriculture, good order, and the general progress of society. As for the Montagnards, they thought that political democracy was not viable in a country where differences in wealth were enormous. Their ideal was a society of small landowners and artisans. Certainly we cannot rule out calculation from their conduct—the more buyers of national property there were, the more numerous were the defenders of the new regime—but it was political calculation and (so to speak) a defensive mechanism. Clearly, however, it was as if everything were done with the avowed intent that a modest sacrifice could serve to prevent a mass movement by the rural proletariat and would assure the continued sale of property at auction which had brought the greater share of national property into the hands of the middle class and well-to-do peasants. But the generosity or cunning of the Revolutionary assemblies would have been insufficient to guarantee this result. Their measures helped stem the peasant tide, but could not have halted it had it risen to a flood. The explanation for the weakness of the peasant attack must be sought in the agrarian conditions of the old regime.

VIII

In concluding this short account, we must first repeat that the Revolution took up the work of the old regime with vigor. By creating the legal conditions for modern, progressive, commercial, capitalist agriculture, it confirmed a trend that had begun long before. By expanding the extent of small property and small farms, it probably slowed the innovations which it had authorized in law, but accentuated

the characteristic feature of the agrarian complexion of France, reinforced the chances for social equilibrium, and slightly diminished the
suffering that technical progress imposed on the poor.

On the other hand, we note that the Revolution was far more moderate than it might have been. Had the wishes of the majority of
peasants been realized, all large-scale property, all the great holdings,
would have been broken up. We need not consider here whether this
would have proved a calamity. We will only observe that the Revolutionaries could not have stood against such action by will-power alone
and that France was in fact saved from it by its own history. Let us
recognize the limitations of this great agrarian transformation, which
created no abyss between the new and the old France.

SUGGESTIONS FOR ADDITIONAL READING

Marc Bloch, "La lutte pour l'individualisme agraire dans la France du
XVIIIᵉ siècle," *Mélanges historiques,* Vol. II (Paris, 1963).

Georges Lefebvre, *Les paysans du Nord Pendant la Révolution française,*
Lille, 1924.

————, *Questions agraires au temps de la terreur,* La-Roche-sur-Yon, 1952.
2nd edition.

————, "La Révolution française et les paysans," *Études sur la Révolution
française* (Paris, 1954).

PAST AND PRESENT: SURVIVALS IN
FRENCH AGRICULTURE *

Marc Bloch

*Through a "historical paradox," the Revolutionary land settle-
ment, by assuring the existence of the peasant small farmer, helped
perpetuate the traditional agrarian structure. The following selection
describes the latter's persistence until well into the nineteenth century,*

* From *Les caractères originaux de l'histoire rurale française* (Paris: Librairie
Armand Colin, 1960) Vol. I, pp. 243–46. Translated by James Friguglietti. Re-
printed by permission of Routledge & Kegan Paul Ltd. and the University of
California Press, publishers of a forthcoming translation.

particularly in the old open-field regions. Marc Bloch, medievalist and economic historian, was one of the great figures in the recent generation of French scholars.

Peasant communities, especially those in regions of open fields, long remained stubbornly attached to time-honored usages. It was not enough for a farmer to close off his fields; he also had to induce his neighbors to respect the enclosure. Under the July Monarchy [1] the breaching of fences, the traditional punishment inflicted on the encloser by an aggrieved community, was not unknown. In the Haute-Saône Department in 1813, "a guard for each furrow" was supposedly needed in order to protect unenclosed artificial meadows. In the first half of the century, lower courts, basing their judgments on local custom, occasionally refused to uphold bans on foraging rights. Little by little, however, the spread of technical improvements brought increased recognition of individual rights. But enclosure still continued to be very infrequent except in those regions where grazing land was replacing cultivated fields. The greater part of what were once open-field areas have remained "open country" down to our own day, and today's traveler is scarcely less aware of the contrast between "plain" and *bocage* [2] than was the twelfth-century poet Wace. The extent of common pasture has certainly declined, yet in the areas of open fields, especially in those of elongated fields, common pasture rights for many years continued, and still continue in force over a great number of holdings.[3] In 1889 the French parliament suppressed common pasturage entirely in meadow-lands, but in the face of peasant opposition had to reinstate it the following year. In Lorraine, Champagne, Picardy, Franche-Comté, and other provinces, many communes took advantage of the right granted them by law to maintain it on farm and grazing lands. Accustomed in his own country to searching through old documents for traces of collective obligations which had long since disappeared from the soil, the English historian Frederic Seebohm was astonished in 1885 to discover, as if he were looking back in time, the herds of Beauce still wandering through the stubble fields. Under the First Empire the legal abolition of compulsory crop rotation aroused

[1] 1830–1848. [Editor's note.]
[2] See Homans's definition of *woodland* country in the first selection. [Editor's note.]
[3] This was written in 1931. Common pasture has disappeared from the arable regions but communal rights still persist in some woodlands and alpine pastures. [Editor's note.]

much regret. Yet, in fact, it long persisted, nearly as much of a requirement as in the past, and in the regions of elongated fields the practice
has survived down to our own time as an obligation prescribed by the
shape of the holdings and even by social constraint. In spring, on the
plateaus of Lorraine and the plains of Alsace and Burgundy, the three
"seasons" still present a contrast of colors.[4]

Yet almost everywhere new planting has replaced the sparse fallow
grass on land that once would have been left to rest.

When it is written, the story of the conquest of the fallow by
crops, a fresh triumph of man over the earth that is as significant as
the great land clearing of the Middle Ages, will undoubtedly be one
of the noblest that can be told. At present the material for it is lacking.
We can faintly discern a few of the forces that spurred the movement:
the introduction of industrial crops; the discovery of chemical fertilizers which, by solving the problem of manure, loosened the historic
association of cereals and cattle and liberated farming from its dependence on fodder crops (the production of which in great quantities
had seemed to men of the eighteenth century to be the necessary and
often formidable precondition for agricultural improvement), rational
specialization of soil, favored by the development of first a European,
then a world economy based on trade; and, lastly, the strides of trade
of another order, that of ideas, which from that time forward united
small rural communities with the more advanced and vigorous areas.

One other fact is certain—that the rhythm of change, naturally
quite different from one region to another, was slow everywhere. Even
in the second half of the nineteenth century more than one countryside, especially in eastern France, still revealed its *sombres* or *somarts,*
untilled lands frequented by shepherds and hunters. In the final analysis, however, save in those areas condemned by nature to hopeless
sterility, farmers have gradually grown accustomed to taking a crop
from the soil almost every year. But, on the average, yields have remained below those of many foreign countries. Virtually everywhere
in the European or Europeanized world, agriculture is becoming more
rational and scientific, adopting technical and financial methods greatly
similar to those of large-scale industry. France has followed along un-
certainly and, in general, has lagged behind most of her neighbors in
this development, which is one of the most prominent features of
contemporary economic life. Even where that aspect of progress in

---

[4] Similarly, bans upon mowing, reaping, and grape harvesting are still legal.
It seems that only the last continue to have any real practical importance.

trade, monoculture, has triumphed—in the winegrowing areas, but more notably and especially in grazing lands—the French peasant, unlike his American counterpart, continues to live at least in part on the produce of his own garden and poultry yard, and often of his own cows and pigs as well. Several reasons can be found for this allegiance to the past, but the one that strikes our eyes immediately is physical. The old pattern of landholdings in the open regions, particularly in those of elongated fields which represent some of the richest areas, has scarcely changed in its basic features. It continues to sustain and re-impose the agrarian habits for which it was intended. Much thought has been given to redistributing land, but a general redistribution of holdings could only be carried out from above. Though the dictatorially minded Marat did not shrink from the idea of such coercion, how could the members of the Constituent Assembly and Convention, and later economists and men in power have followed him? Respect for the independence of landowners was at the base of their social philosophy. Could any crueler blow to the rights of a proprietor be imagined than to force him to renounce his hereditary fields? Need-less to say, the rural masses, whose reaction could hardly fail to influ-ence even those regimes not based on free suffrage, would certainly have resisted an upheaval of such magnitude. In fact, land redistribu-tion, which we might have expected to find accomplished by persua-sion, has always been most uncommon. Through a strange historical paradox, the same reverence for individual property which led re-formers to reject the old principles of community responsibility barred them from taking the decisive step towards redistribution which alone could have broken through the shackles that bound property and has-tened technical progress.

SUGGESTIONS FOR ADDITIONAL READING

Frederic O. Sargent, "The Persistence of Communal Tenure in French Agriculture," *Agricultural History,* Vol. 32, No. 2 (1958).

A. Soboul, "The French Rural Community in the 18th and 19th Centuries," *Past and Present,* No. 10 (1956).

AGRICULTURE IN WESTERN EUROPE:
THE GREAT DEPRESSION 1880–1900 *

Michael Tracy

During the second half of the nineteenth century, farming, free of the feudal pattern and vastly improved by a technological revolution, was in process of transformation into today's commercialized agriculture. At this stage of development, there began the invasion of the European market by cheaper foodstuffs from overseas. The resulting depression in prices and the reaction of the various nations to it are the subject of the selection that follows. Since this period, tariff protection and other forms of government intervention have increasingly influenced agricultural production. Michael Tracy is a British economist specializing in agricultural affairs.

European Agriculture before the Depression

By the middle of the nineteenth century, agriculture in Western Europe had already taken on more or less its present form. The number and size of holdings, the location of farms and farm buildings, the forms of land tenure, were not very different from what they are today. Contrasts between one country and another were already obvious: they were the outcome, firstly, of the various ways in which agriculture had emerged from the typical feudal pattern, whereby most of the land had been arranged in open fields, cultivated by a peasantry owing various rents and services to their lord; secondly, of the extent to which general economic progress had influenced the development of agriculture.

Thus in Britain the enclosure and consolidation of agricultural holdings over a long period led to the creation of comparatively large, unified farms. The landed aristocracy had never been overthrown and indeed played an important role in this process, which they guided to their best advantage: when their feudal power had gone, they still formed an important class of landlords, letting out most of their land

* From *Agriculture in Western Europe* (New York: Frederick A. Praeger, 1964) pp. 19–35. Reprinted by permission of Frederick A. Praeger, Inc., and Jonathan Cape Ltd.

to tenant farmers. The process created another class, that of the landless labourers, many of whom were forced off the land and into the growing towns. This move from the land was stimulated by the Industrial Revolution, in which Britain had a long lead over all other countries, and, as a result, the population living from agriculture formed a smaller proportion of the whole in Britain than in any other country. Further, overall economic progress was reflected in agriculture: the agrarian structure with large farms and a class of wealthy landowners ready to invest in their estates, made British farming particularly receptive to technological progress, and in the middle of the nineteenth century it was the most advanced in the world.

Denmark also had achieved a favourable agricultural structure, but in a different way. Here the abolition of the feudal system took place to the advantage of the peasants, who were encouraged and aided by the government to buy the land they farmed. The result was to create farms not so big as in Britain, but big enough for the needs of the time, and conveniently grouped in single units. A remarkably advanced educational system also contributed to forming an independent and progressive farming community.

In other countries of the Continent, the situation was not so good. In many cases the feudal pattern had been violently broken up by revolutionary movements, and the landlords had been expropriated or compelled to sell. Little was done to ensure that the land taken into the possession of the peasants should be arranged in a rational manner so as to give its new owners a decent living. Thus in France (though many large estates survived the Revolution or were re-created afterwards) the majority of the holdings were so small as to be barely viable: nearly 40 per cent of the agricultural area was in farms of less than 20 hectares (in Britain the corresponding figure was under 20 per cent). The practice of dividing land up between the heirs, on the death of the owner, aggravated the problem, both by reducing the average size of farm and by perpetuating the "fragmentation" of holdings between several separate plots, often at a considerable distance one from another. Similar patterns of land ownership were found in other parts of Western Europe (partly as a result of French occupation during the Napoleonic Wars). In Belgium and parts of West Germany, in particular, there were many small and fragmented farms; in West Germany over half the agricultural area was in holdings of less than 20 hectares. In several other regions of Western Europe—including Switzerland, the Tyrol, and parts of South Germany—the feudal system had already been overthrown in the peasant wars of the thirteenth and fourteenth centuries, and a peasant agriculture was firmly established.

In Eastern Europe the situation was totally different. Even where a degree of emancipation had taken place, it had failed to create a strong peasantry. In the Austro-Hungarian Empire and in Russia, the traditional landed classes remained in power. The new German Empire had in its eastern regions a near-feudal pattern which contrasted sharply with the mainly peasant agriculture of its other regions: the land was still predominantly in the hands of a powerful aristocracy (the "Junkers"), owning large estates worked by hired labour.

In most of the countries of the Continent, by the middle of the century, the Industrial Revolution had hardly begun to influence agriculture. Farming remained the most important occupation; dissatisfied peasants had not much opportunity to move into expanding industries. There was as yet hardly any stimulus for agriculture to improve its methods: transport and communications were deficient, and there was little flow of new ideas into the countryside. Rural education was often rudimentary, and agriculture remained backward.

The pattern of agricultural trade at this time was very different from what it was to be a few decades later. Generally trade remained unimportant in relation to production. Britain, as a result of its expanding industrial population, had already become a large importer of food; but these imports, in spite of the repeal of the Corn Laws in 1846, hardly constituted a serious danger for British agriculture. France imported some grains, especially wheat, and exported others. Germany imported grain for the consuming and livestock-producing areas of the west, and exported wheat and rye from the great estates of the east. Denmark at this time also exported grain: her export trade in livestock products had scarcely begun. The largest exporter of grain in the world was Russia.

Agricultural trade was thus very largely an intra-European affair. The advance of technology had not yet reached the stage when the agricultural produce of the New World could be transported quickly and cheaply by land and by sea. European agriculture, on the whole, was still untroubled by outside competition.

The Growth in Competition

The main cause of the subsequent transformation of the agricultural scene was the immense increase in imports of cheap grain coming from

North America and also to some extent from Russia. This was the result of the opening up of virgin lands and of revolutionary improvements in methods of transport. In North America especially the availability of vast land resources made possible extremely cheap production, and from the middle of the century steadily increasing use was made of farm machinery—reapers, binders, and, later, efficient combine harvesters. Russia's advantage lay in having plenty of land and cheap labour.

In the 1850's American railways began to tap the Great Plains, and by 1884 the Rockies could be reached by seven different railway routes in the United States or Canada. In Russia, too, new railways brought grain to ports on the Baltic and the Black Sea. At the same time there was rapid progress in shipping: in the second half of the century ships began to be built not with wood but with iron, later with steel, and this made possible a great increase in their size and carrying capacity. In addition, sail gave way to steam, and the compound engine, which greatly reduced fuel costs, came into use from the 1860's. During the 1870's and 1880's, the cost of transporting wheat both by rail from Chicago to New York and by steamer from New York to Liverpool was cut by about half. The price of American wheat arriving in Liverpool fell by even more than the amount of the reduction in transport costs.

The effect of these technical developments might have been felt even sooner but for the Crimean War of 1853–56, which closed the Baltic and the Black Sea to Russian exports, and the American Civil War of 1861–64, which curbed U.S. exports to Europe. The peace which prevailed in America and Europe for forty years after the Franco-German War of 1870–71 provided the conditions necessary for a great expansion of trade.

From 1877 North America had the benefit of four consecutive seasons in which harvests were excellent. In Western Europe, on the other hand, these were bad years: the harvest of 1879 was disastrous. Previously, small crops had been accompanied by higher prices which helped to maintain returns to farmers. Now, however, exports from the United States rose sharply, doubling within a few years: prices in Europe fell instead of rising, and farmers suffered severe losses. From then on grain prices fell steadily. The whole period from about 1873 to 1896 was one of general economic depression and falling prices, which aggravated the problems of agriculture.

In the late 1880's, American grain exports for a time ceased to rise, and there was a slight recovery in prices. But the 1890's brought a renewed crisis. In 1891 the United States had a record crop and exports once again rose substantially. At about the same time Russia was increasing its exports, Canada was beginning to make an impact on the world market, and the Suez Canal was facilitating trade from India and Australia. Grain prices fell once more in 1892, and in 1895 they reached their lowest point: the world price of wheat was then little more than half the pre-depression level.

Reduced wheat crops in 1895 and 1896, partly due to some contraction in the wheat area in response to the lower prices, helped to relieve the pressure. At the same time, rising production costs in the United States made themselves felt: by about 1890 all the productive land had been occupied and the price of land began to rise. Also, domestic consumption in the United States was rising. Grain prices thus recovered gradually from about 1896 onwards, helped by a general improvement in the economic situation. By the turn of the century the agricultural depression had spent its force, and the years leading up to the First World War were favourable to farmers in both North America and Europe.

In its early stages, the crisis affected mainly the grain market. Later on, techniques of refrigeration began to be applied on a commercial scale: the United States started to ship frozen meat in 1875, Australia in 1877, and shipments grew enormously from then on. However, production of livestock products was rising much less rapidly than that of grains, while with the gradual improvement in the standard of living the demand for livestock products was increasing comparatively fast. The result was that the decline in the prices of meat and other livestock products was never as large as that which occurred for grains. The experience of Britain is a useful guide, since the British market remained free: the prices of livestock products began to fall only in 1885, some five years later than the beginning of the crisis for grains, and at the worst of the depression, in 1896, livestock prices were about three-quarters of their pre-depression level when crop prices were little more than a half.

This difference in the trend of prices as between crop and livestock products is of considerable significance. It means in the first place that the effects of the depression were not felt equally by arable farmers and by livestock producers. The former suffered directly from the reduced value of their produce. The latter also suffered a fall in value, but it came later and was not so serious; moreover, they *benefited* from the much greater fall in the price of feed grains.

It follows that the best policy for European countries during the Great Depression was to carry out a shift from crop production to livestock. Countries which were able and far-sighted enough to do this stood a much better chance of overcoming the crisis than those which, in the face of the new trends, persevered with former habits.

The difference in price trends also leads to a distinction between large and small farms in a given country. Returns per unit of land tend to be smaller with crops, so that profitable crop production requires a fairly large area: grain farming is therefore carried out mainly on the larger holdings. The smaller farms—peasant holdings in particular—generally depend for their livelihood on dairy cows, pigs, and poultry; they may produce some grain and other fodder for the use of their own livestock, but they often need to purchase additional supplies. It was therefore the larger farms which were most affected by the crisis.

In some cases the distinction is also geographical. This was particularly so in Germany, with many large grain-producing estates in East Prussia. In England, arable farms were found mainly in East Anglia and parts of the south, while in the north and west livestock farming predominated. In France, the plains of the Paris basin were the principal grain-producing region.

These differences are important for an understanding of the Great Depression. At this time the farmers best able to make their views known and to exert an influence on official policy were the larger farmers, particularly when they belonged to a ruling aristocracy; the peasants were generally unorganized and unrepresented. This suggests that the traditional view of the Great Depression may exaggerate its severity. Too much emphasis is usually laid on the fall in grain prices and on the unfavourable consequences for arable farmers; not enough attention has been paid to the much less difficult situation of livestock producers.

It also follows that when various European countries introduced measures of protection, they did so largely at the instigation of the bigger farmers and for their benefit, and that for the peasantry the advantages of protection were much less evident.

The Free Trade Interlude

For a short period before the Great Depression, trade between European countries became more nearly free from tariffs and other restrictions than at any other time in history. The impetus came from

Britain, where the Free Trade movement had gathered strength throughout the early nineteenth century and achieved its most spectacular success in the repeal of the Corn Laws in 1846. This movement drew its inspiration from the teaching of Adam Smith and his disciples, but it corresponded also to the commercial interests of Britain at the time: with undisputed leadership in industry and commerce, Britain had everything to gain and nothing to lose from the greatest possible freedom of trade.

Having committed herself to free trade, Britain therefore sought to induce other countries to follow along the same path. The liberal doctrines of the Manchester School were not unknown in Continental countries, but the inferiority of their industry as compared with that of Britain made protection seem essential. Somewhat unexpectedly, Britain found an ally in France: Napoleon III, who in 1852 had established himself as emperor, with extensive powers, was favourably disposed towards free trade. He was moreover anxious, for political reasons, to establish close relations with Britain. In 1860, against the opposition of his Parliament, he signed the Anglo-French Treaty of Commerce.

This treaty was of significance not only for the reductions it brought about in French duties (and the comparatively minor concessions by Britain), but also for its consequences as the cornerstone of a series of subsequent treaties between France and practically all other European countries. Each of these was based on the "most favoured nation" principle, so that the concessions granted to one country were automatically extended to the others. Thus, throughout most of Europe, trade was freed or subjected only to mild duties.

Trade in agricultural products became even more free than that in manufactures. By 1860 Britain had abolished duties not only on grain but on almost all other agricultural imports, leaving only a few revenue duties. France practically removed agricultural protection in the 1860 treaty, and in 1861 abolished her sliding scale of grain duties. Farmers in Germany were still interested mainly in exporting grain and therefore wanted free trade: the Zollverein's duties on grain had been abolished in 1853. In Italy the moderate Piedmontese duties formed the basis of the tariff for the unified kingdom, and after treaties with France and other countries, agriculture was protected only by low duties on grains. Belgium in 1871 decreed free entry for the main foodstuffs. The Netherlands dropped its grain duties in 1862. In most other countries agricultural trade was free or nearly so.

The Protectionist Revival

The subsequent return to protection took place gradually and had a number of causes. One of these was the Franco-German War of 1870, and the nationalist sentiment to which it gave rise in both countries. Another, closely associated with this, was the increasing concern with industrial development throughout the Continent; demands by industrialists for protection became more insistent, demonstrating that they at least had never been converted to free trade. Public opinion became increasingly willing to listen to them. These demands were accentuated as prices began a long downward trend, starting in 1873 and lasting till about 1896, with only a short respite from 1880 to 1882; this depression kept wages and profits low and reduced purchasing power. The protectionist movement, especially in Germany, was able to draw inspiration and justification from Friedrich List's school of nationalist economics, with its stress on economic development through protection. Thus, when European agriculture was awakened to the challenge of overseas competition, there was ample scope for powerful protectionist alliances between industrial and agricultural interests.

In France the reversal of policy was marked by the tariff of 1881, which introduced moderate protection for industry and made large increases in the duties on livestock and livestock products. In 1885 and 1887 the duties on all major agricultural products were very substantially raised. The Méline Tariff of 1892 gave increased protection to both industry and agriculture. These measures remained substantially unchanged up to the First World War: in 1910 a modernized tariff brought some increase in protection for industry, but no important change in agricultural duties.

Germany's reconversion to protection began with the tariff of 1879, which restored duties on various manufactures and also imposed moderate duties on agricultural products. In 1885 and 1887 there were further and substantial increases in the grain duties. This protectionist policy was the work of Bismarck: after his dismissal in 1890, Germany for a while followed the opposite course. Germany's need by then was to obtain expanded markets for her industrial exports, and in a series of commercial treaties Bismarck's successors made limited reductions in the agricultural duties in return for advantages for German exports. But this led to violent opposition from the farming sector and in particular from the powerful Prussian landowners. It also gave rise to violent controversy as to the desirability of Germany's becoming an increasingly industrial nation. Satisfaction was finally given to the agricultural interests with the tariff of 1902.

Italy re-established protection in 1878, mainly with the object of protecting her infant industries, but the duties were moderate because of the desire not to provoke retaliation against Italy's agricultural exports. Various revisions were made in subsequent years. The main change in policy occurred with the tariff of 1887, which raised the duties on both industrial and agricultural products. By then industrialists had become increasingly sensitive to foreign competition, while grain-producing farmers were suffering from the universal fall in prices. The producers of export commodities—wine, olive oil, fruit, vegetables—had little competition to fear and did not want foreign countries to discriminate against their exports, but as in other countries the large grain producers were the most influential. One of the first results of the 1887 tariff was in fact sharp retaliation by France; there followed a tariff war between the two countries lasting till 1892, and normal trade relations were not restored till 1899. This brought great hardship to agricultural exporting interests in Italy. Meanwhile the grain producers succeeded in having the duty on wheat raised by successive stages from 3 lire per 100 kg. in 1887 to 7.50 lire in 1898. The protectionist revival in Italy was accompanied by a tendency for the school of national economics on the German model to prevail over economists of the Manchester School: from 1875 the former made its voice heard in the *Giornale degli Economisti*, while an Adam Smith Society was formed and published the *Economista*, but became less and less effective.

Once Belgium became firmly established as an independent nation (its secession from the Netherlands took place in 1830), she realized that, as an industrial nation heavily dependent on foreign trade, her interests lay in the greatest possible freedom of trade. But here too the agricultural crisis caused a revival of protectionist agitation and led in 1887 to the imposition of tariffs on livestock and meat. The protection involved remained moderate. In 1895 the duties on a number of agricultural products were raised, but grains (other than oats) remained free.

Economic policy in Switzerland was originally dominated by the liberalism of the Manchester School, and the Constitution of 1874 did not allow the Confederation to intervene in economic matters. Switzerland's trade policy was to obtain advantages for her exports of manufactured goods by offering an open market in agricultural products. Swiss farmers themselves were for a time inclined to favour free trade, because of their interest in exporting cheese and breeding cattle. But when the crisis broke they too began to demand protection. Though in 1884 and 1887 some duties were imposed on manufactured products, no immediate satisfaction was given to the farmers, except for an increase in the subsidies granted for various purposes. Protection for agriculture was first introduced with the tariff of 1891. Like the Belgian tariff, this left grains largely unprotected: grains were only a small part of total Swiss agricultural output but they were a large import item, and duties would have weighed heavily on consumers and on users of feed grains. Another feature of the tariff was that the large dairy sector could not be given direct protection, because cheese exports formed an important outlet for this sector and the price of cheese on export markets largely determined the whole price structure for dairy products. The tariff thus concentrated protection on beef cattle and meat, and it was hoped that this would give some indirect help to the dairy sector by diverting part of the milk supplies to feeding more calves. The agricultural duties were raised in the 1902 tariff and modified by treaties in 1905.

From the late 1870's onwards, measures of protection for both agriculture and industry were adopted also by Austria-Hungary, Sweden, Spain, and Portugal, while Russia and the United States sheltered their growing industries behind prohibitive tariff walls; in the United States the McKinley Tariff of 1890 extended protection to agriculture, with increased duties on grains and new duties on some other products.

This left a few European countries holding determinedly to free trade principles, the most important of these being Britain.

Agriculture in Britain was no less subject to overseas competition than that of other European countries. In fact a large sector of British agriculture was ruined in the course of the depression; many agricultural workers moved to the towns and much arable land was turned over to grass. "High farming" gave way to the utmost economy in operations and even to neglect. Yet the British Government refused the slightest degree of protection. Moreover, there was no effective move for protection among the farmers themselves. It was only after the end of the agricultural depression, from about 1903 to 1905, that a vigorous campaign for "Tariff Reform" was started, but this was based on the desire to secure preferences for Empire trade rather than on the wish to protect British agriculture (indeed, the conflict between the two aims was never satisfactorily reconciled).

Denmark too held firmly to free trade, but while in Britain the policy was one of pure laissez-faire, Denmark's reaction to overseas competition was to carry out a fundamental transformation of its agriculture. There was a large shift from crops to livestock production, and Danish exports of livestock products became established on the British and German markets.

Developments in the Netherlands were similar to those in Denmark. The importance of foreign trade to the economy had led to a long-standing attachment to free trade principles. When the unprotected Dutch market came to be swamped with foreign goods to which other markets were increasingly closed, and when unemployment began to rise in consequence, a protectionist movement made itself heard. The Government nevertheless withstood these demands. The national Agricultural Council declared that proposals to raise the grain duties would do no good to agriculture, as increasing the duties would remove the incentive to work and lead to many protective measures which would raise prices of agricultural inputs; it also considered that the situation in the Netherlands under free trade was no worse than in countries which had already adopted protection. This energetic refusal put an end to protectionist claims for agriculture: the farmers thereupon accepted the free-trade policy, set up associations to improve the processing of their products, and made use of the training institutes set up by the Government. A justification for this policy could be found in the subsequent increase in exports of livestock products, fruit, and vegetables.

It is not easy to give a general idea of the degree of protection for agriculture attained in the course of the Great Depression. Practically all tariff rates were "specific" (i.e., in terms of weight or quantity), and to express them in *ad valorem* terms involves difficulties in selecting appropriate price data. . . . However, it seems reasonable to conclude that in most of the countries which had adopted protection for agriculture, the degree of protection before the First World War lay somewhere between 20 and 30 per cent.

Factors Influencing the Choice of Policies

The preceding pages have shown the wide divergence in the policies followed during the Great Depression. In most countries, including in particular France and Germany, there was a purely defensive reaction, taking the form of greatly increased tariff protection. Britain held to laissez-faire, and an adjustment was forced on agriculture in the form of contraction and decline in the arable sector. In Denmark and the Netherlands, on the other hand, there was a positive response, characterized by the absence of defensive measures and a deliberate adaptation and improvement of agricultural production and marketing.

What was responsible for these differences? It seems that a considerable number of factors played a role. Perhaps the first was the general attitude in each country towards economic policy and in particular to trade. Britain, with its early start in the Industrial Revolution, had a clear advantage in the maximum freedom of trade. Small countries like Denmark, Belgium, and the Netherlands, with a shortage of natural resources, were heavily dependent on trade and favoured free trade for that reason. France and Germany, on the other hand, wanted to develop their industries and needed protection to do so; with their extensive domestic resources they could afford to restrict trade (at least up to the point when, in the case of Germany, markets had to be found for industrial exports).

Economic theory played a part, but probably only a small part, in shaping public attitudes. There is no doubt that List was the dominant influence on academic thinking in Germany, as Smith and Ricardo were in Britain, and their respective theories provided powerful arguments for the opposing camps of Protectionists and Free Traders. But Kindleberger, in a study of the different responses to the agricultural depression, rightly observes:

It might be fair to say that the economists of Britain and the national economists of Germany provided the rationale for the action taken rather than its impetus. And the relative unimportance of this function may be indicated by the action of France and Italy, taken in the absence of any distinctive rationale.[1]

The extent of public willingness to support agriculture was another important factor. Prevailing opinions were composed of elements of both reasoning and sentiment. The resort to agricultural protectionism in both France and Germany owed much to a widespread belief in the virtues of rural life and in the disadvantages of a high degree of industrialization. In France this sentiment was expressed in an extreme

[1] C. P. Kindleberger, "Group behavior and international trade," *Journal of Political Economy*, February 1951, p. 37.

(but vague) form by Jules Méline, particularly in his book *Le retour à la terre*. In Germany, discussion on this point took the form of an academic debate on the "Agrar-oder Industriestaat" issue, and the arguments of Professor Adolf Wagner, the main advocate of the "Agrarstaat," carried great weight: he stressed the social disadvantages of the rise in the urban population and the risks—which were not only strategic—of excessive dependence on food imports.

On the other hand, the main argument working against public willingness to protect agriculture was the effect on food prices. In Britain, the successful campaign against the Corn Laws had left a deeply engrained hostility to any form of tax on foodstuffs: "cheap bread" remained a powerful rallying cry. In other countries, this was an argument frequently used by Free Traders, but with little success.

The strategic argument—the need to ensure self-sufficiency in food supplies in time of war—was part of the general case for an "Agrarstaat" and was frequently advanced in almost all countries as a justification for protection. This argument certainly played a role, but perhaps less than is sometimes thought: it was an additional reason for statesmen to satisfy pressure from agricultural interests, rather than an independent factor influencing policy. Perhaps it manifested itself most clearly in reverse: there is no doubt that a vital factor in Britain's indifference to the fact of her agriculture was her undisputed mastery of the seas and her possession of rich food-producing colonies.

These factors outside agriculture helped to determine the possibilities for forming protective alliances between industrial and agricultural interests. At critical stages in France, Germany, and Italy, such alliances were responsible for restoring protection to both industry and agriculture. This union could be maintained only so long as the common interest in obtaining protection was stronger than conflicts of interest in other respects. Some such conflict between the two sectors was always inevitable. Protection for industry was liable to raise the cost of farm tools and equipment, possibly also of farm wages. Protection for agriculture might, by raising food prices, cause increased labour costs for industry; it might also raise the price of raw materials. This last problem was usually not serious, since agricultural raw materials for industry were generally produced overseas and not by European agriculture; but an important exception was wool, and it is significant that, even in the countries where agricultural protection went furthest, wool was generally left entirely free from duty, and the result of competition from Australia, South America, and South Africa was a drastic fall in the sheep population of Europe. Conflict was inevitable also when industry was concerned with enlarging its export markets: in Germany this problem became acute in the 1890's, and the fact that it was resolved in favour of agriculture demonstrates the political strength of the farmers.

The influence of the farming community was to a large extent a question of the relative size of the agricultural population: the contrast between Britain and the other countries needs no comment. It was also determined by the extent to which general democratic evolution had deprived the rural aristocracy of its power. In Britain the political reforms starting with the 1832 Reform Act had dethroned the landed classes; moreover, the division of interests and outlook between landlords and tenants, and also between arable and livestock farmers, prevented the formation of any coherent agricultural pressure group. Denmark was a land of small-to-medium farms, with a highly developed democracy. But in countries where there remained a dominant class of large landowners (often interested primarily in the price of grain), this group was able to present itself as the representative of the whole agricultural interest, regardless of the real needs of other groups in agriculture, and to exert considerable influence over the course of official policy. Thus in Germany the Junkers remained a coherent group with vestiges of feudal power and an entrenched position in the state, in France the campaign for protection was led by the aristocratic Société des Agriculteurs de France, and in Italy by the big grain producers.

SUGGESTIONS FOR ADDITIONAL READING

Michel Augé-Laribé, *La politique agricole de la France de 1880 à 1940*, Paris, 1950.

J. H. Clapham, *The Economic Development of France and Germany 1815–1914*, Cambridge, 1945. 4th edition.

Shepard B. Clough, *The Economic History of Modern Italy*, New York, 1964.

Alexander Gerschenkron, *Bread and Democracy in Germany*, Berkeley and Los Angeles, 1943.

Heinz Haushofer, *Die Dieutsche Landwirtschaft im Technischen Zeitalter*, Stuttgart, 1963.

E. Jensen, *Danish Agriculture—Its Economic Development*, Copenhagen, 1937.

Christabel S. Orwin and Edith H. Whetham, *History of British Agriculture, 1846–1914,* London, 1964.

Zeger W. Sneller, *Geschiedenis van de Nederlandse landbouw 1795–1940,* Groningen, 1951.

LAND TENURE AND LAND REFORM IN MODERN RUSSIA *

Lazar Volin

Serfdom and the low level of general economic progress accounted for a Russian agriculture that, by Western standards, was still primitive at the middle of the nineteenth century. The freeing of the serfs in 1861 represented only half a step forward. The selection that follows shows how, after 1861, agrarian and constitutional reform became closely linked and explains why the peasant question still remained a burning one on the eve of the Revolution. Lazar Volin has written on the agrarian history of Tsarist and Soviet Russia and is one of the outstanding authorities on Soviet agriculture in this country. He is currently Chief, East European Branch, Foreign Regional Analysis Division, United States Department of Agriculture.

Few countries have had such varied experience with the problem of land tenure and land reform as Russia during the past hundred years.[1] Within this period Russian peasantry, i.e., the great mass of the Russian population, has passed through the whole gamut of changes in the agrarian structure: serfdom, liberation, and agrarian reforms, revolutions, counter-revolutions and, at last, but let us hope not finally, a sort of a new enslavement to the State in the kolkhoz, the collective farm. The one central thread in this history that is never completely lost is the contest of the peasant with the land-owning nobility and its protector, the Tsarist government. This contest gave way, after 1917, to a struggle between the peasant and the Communist state. In the course

* From *Agricultural History,* Vol. 27, No. 2 (1953). Reprinted by permission of The Agricultural History Society and the author.

[1] A paper read at the joint session of the Agricultural History Society and the American Historical Association, in Washington, D.C., December 28, 1952.

of the peasant-landlord contest, the government was confronted, on several occasions, with a dilemma—agrarian reform or revolution—which was resolved now one way, now the other.

Nearly a hundred years ago, while serfdom still prevailed in Russia, Tsar Alexander II recognized this dilemma. He warned the serf-owning landlords that it would be better to liberate the serfs from above than to wait until they liberated themselves. It was a timely warning. For discontent was growing among the Russian peasantry, as was opposition to serfdom among the intelligentsia, nurtured, as it was, on Western liberal and humanitarian ideas. The disastrous defeat in the Crimean War (1854–55) of the reactionary regime of Tsar Nicholas I, father of Alexander II, had already revealed the bankruptcy of the whole social system rooted in serfdom. Alexander read the handwriting on the wall and, despite opposition of the great majority of the influential serf-owning landlord class, chose the path of reform. The result was the famous Emancipation Manifesto of 1861, abolishing serfdom in Russia forever and opening a new era justly known as that of the Great Reforms.

However, the Russian peasant question was not solved by the Emancipation, as it was largely settled in Western Europe by the French Revolution and the subsequent agrarian reforms. Already, in the 1870's, the depressed condition of the liberated peasantry began to cause public and even official concern. This concern mounted as time went on, reaching a state of virtual alarm at the turn of the century. The peasant question, as the voluminous literature devoted to it attests, had truly become a burning national issue, especially after the peasantry shifted from passive suffering and discontent to rebellion in 1905, which foreshadowed the agrarian revolution of 1917.

Thus, forty years after Alexander II's far-reaching and promising agrarian reform, the country was faced with a severe agrarian crisis. Now, what were the causes of the crisis? What lessons can we learn from this experience that would be useful today, when international attention is focused on the problem of land reform in the underdeveloped countries of Asia and Africa—a problem that has become crucial in the contest between democracy and the survivals of feudalism, on the one hand, and Soviet Communism in propaganda and action, on the other?

The Emancipation reform of the 1860's was based on sound principles: 1) The liberated peasants were to become small land proprietors. They were to be allotted holdings from land owned by their masters that would enable them to gain a livelihood and to pay taxes and the purchase price of the land. Thus, a landless proletariat, a tenant peasantry, was to be avoided. 2) The government was to pay the landlords a fair price for the land allotted to the liberated peasants and collect it from the latter, over a long-term period in installments, so-called redemption payments. 3) Landlords were to receive no payment for liberating the person of the serf.

However, under the pressure of the land-owning class, which was influential at the imperial court and in the higher ranks of bureaucracy, the Emancipation legislation and its implementation had deviated more or less widely from these basic principles. And from these deviations stemmed most of the difficulties that bedeviled the post-Emancipation period of Russian agrarian history. This is a theme which I have only time to sketch briefly, omitting for the most part statistical and other details.

To begin with, a large group of the peasants were deprived of some of the land that they had tilled under serfdom. Many of them had more time once they were free from compulsory work on their former masters' estates, but less land of their own to cultivate. This was particularly the case in the fertile black-soil region of European Russia where land was valuable to the landlords. In a large part of this region the area allotted to the liberated peasants was reduced by more than one-fourth, compared to their holdings under serfdom. In some provinces 40 per cent and more of such land was kept by the landlords on Emancipation.[2]

However, where the interests of the land-owning nobles were not involved, as in the case of peasants owned by the imperial family, and particularly the so-called state-owned peasants, the terms of land allotment were more generous. Likewise, in the western provinces the peasants fared better during the Emancipation, for here most of the landowners were Poles who became *personae non gratae* as a result of the Polish insurrection of 1863. Nevertheless, the central fact cannot be denied that a large segment of the Russian peasantry gained its freedom with a niggardly endowment of land. The adverse effect of this loss of land on peasants' well-being became increasingly manifest with the rapid growth of population following Emancipàtion.

But in the beginning other shortcomings were more important

[2] P. I. Lyashchenko, *History of the National Economy of Russia to the 1917 Revolution,* translated by L. M. Herman, introduction by Calvin B. Hoover (New York, 1949), 382–84.

than the smallness of the allotments. Landlords frequently retained the better land so the peasants were given land of inferior quality. Holdings were often also inconveniently situated. In some cases they were a long distance from the village; in others the peasant holding was accessible only by passage through the property of the landlord, which created a source of endless friction to plague the future peasant-landlord relations. The peasant holding frequently also lacked various essential elements of a well-balanced farm, such as pasture, forest, and water supply. Shortage of pasture adversely affected livestock, and, consequently, the supply of manure needed to fertilize the fields. Lack of forests meant that the inadequate forage supply of the peasant farm was diminished further by diversion of straw for fuel. To avoid such consequences, the peasants had to lease land from their former masters, often on onerous terms, again becoming economically dependent on the landlords.

Here, then, is the first object lesson of Russian agrarian reform: not only the size of the holding, but also the quality of the land and the location and balanced character of the holding, are important if the peasant is really to be an independent proprietor and if economic dependence on the large landowner is to be avoided.

In financial arrangements, as in the matter of land allotment, there was also a wide gap between the principles and the reality of emancipation settlement. The peasants were saddled with heavy redemption payments, which, in many cases, concealed illegal compensation for personal liberation. These payments often exceeded the market value of the allotted land at the time of the Emancipation. Furthermore, to the redemption payments were added high taxes and labor duties that earned the peasantry the invidious distinction of being the most heavily tax-burdened class of prerevolutionary Russia. And in order to make the peasants bear this heavy load and to insure the collection of redemption payments and taxes by the state, serious restrictions were placed on the peasants' civil and property rights.

The liberated Russian peasant, therefore, was not a full-fledged citizen or a fully independent land proprietor. The mir, or village community, which usually included peasant families who had been owned at the time of serfdom by the same master, was entrusted with the collective responsibility for the assessment and payment of the peasants' obligations to the state. This involved the burdensome practice of joint unlimited liability of all members of the mir for the tax obligations of each. For this purpose the mir was provided with wide police powers and discretionary authority over the peasant's life and property, which resulted in much abuse and oppression of the individual. The peasant could not legally sell his allotted land, nor could he refuse to accept it. He could not leave the village even temporarily without the consent of the mir, which could refuse to issue or renew that *sine qua non,* the passport. Thus, in many respects, the peasant exchanged one master, the landlord, for another one, the mir. It may be added that, while a thorough and enlightened judiciary reform was enacted in Russia in the 1860's, which resulted in peasants serving on juries in higher courts, these peasants, nevertheless, were subject to the jurisdiction of their own separate lower courts. These courts used so-called customary uncodified law that resulted in much arbitrariness, and they retained corporal punishment, which had been abolished as a penalty in the general courts.

With some exceptions, the ownership of allotted land was vested in the mir and not in the individual peasant or peasant family. Under this system each peasant family was allotted, on some uniform basis, a holding (consisting usually of a number of non-contiguous scattered strips or plots) which it cultivated independently, unlike the present Soviet collective farming. Over a large part of Russia the mir system involved periodic or occasional repartition of land holdings in order to adjust them to changes in the membership of the mir. Such land repartition, or redistribution, was also often stimulated during the post-Emancipation period by the need to readjust the fiscal burden among the different peasant families. The result was further fragmentation of the non-contiguous peasant holdings and instability of tenure, which were inimical to agricultural progress.

The second lesson of Russian experience with agrarian reform plainly emerges: Mere allotment of land to small holders is a dubious economic procedure if the land is overpriced and overtaxed. Particularly is this true when rapid growth of rural population, as in nineteenth-century Russia, leads to further diminution and fragmentation of holdings—a process which was encouraged by the repartitional and fiscal systems. A distinguished Russian statistician, Professor Kaufman, estimated that, by the end of the nineteenth century, the peasant holdings in a number of regions of European Russia had, on the average, a little over half, or half, and in other regions less than half, of the land that had been allotted to them during the Emancipation.[3]

[3] A. A. Kaufman, *Agrarnyi Vopros v Rossii* [*The Agrarian Question in Russia*] (2nd ed., Moscow, 1918), 44–45.

And it became customary to speak of overpopulation in the central black soil area of European Russia; though scholars usually qualified the concept by the term "relative" overpopulation, i.e., relative to the prevailing state of farm technique.

Rural overpopulation—"too many people on too little land"—is only too well known in many of the underdeveloped countries. But it seems a paradox in the case of Russia, where, during the second half of the nineteenth century, there was still considerable free land for agricultural settlement; though the total area of land suitable for cultivation then, as now, should not be exaggerated, as it is much less than one may assume by looking at the enormous territory of the country on the map.

However, migration of rural population to sparsely settled areas was discouraged by the government during the first two post-Emancipation decades for fear of depriving landowners of a cheap labor supply. The poverty of the Russian peasant and his inability to dispose legally of his allotted land also hindered migration. To be sure, all this did not prevent peasant farmers from infiltrating new regions. You will no doubt recall that the great Russian historian, Kluchevsky, stressed continuous colonization as "the basic fact" in Russian history. Still, large systematic migration, requiring considerable capital investment, did not begin until the end of the nineteenth century, especially after the construction of the Siberian Railroad. Then the government changed its policy and began to assist and encourage resettlement on a large scale.

It is true that, in many cases, there was another way for the Russian peasant to overcome the shortage of land: namely, a transition to a more intensive, more productive farming, with higher returns per acre and per man. It was the path followed by small farmers in Western Europe. But agricultural intensification on a western pattern usually requires some capital, a knowledge of improved agricultural methods, personal initiative, and security of land tenure. And, of course, it is greatly helped by industrialization, which expands the markets for the products of intensive agriculture and provides a new ocupational outlet for any surplus rural population. But practically all of these factors were lacking or only weakly developed in Russia during the second half of the nineteenth century. Industrial revolution began in earnest in Russia only towards the close of that century. Personal initiative was stifled by the atmosphere of regimentation and administrative oppression. I have already alluded to the insecurity of the repartitional tenure. And where could the Russian peasants, crushed as they were by the heavy burden of redemption payments and taxes, obtain capital needed to improve their farming, when, moreover, practically the only source of credit was the village usurer—the original "kulak" or fist? And how were the largely illiterate peasants to obtain knowledge of improved agricultural methods, without organized technical assistance and education? The failure of the Tsarist government to foster education during the second half of the nineteenth century was notorious. It failed not only to spread technical agronomic knowledge, but even to stamp out illiteracy, though Russian experience provides abundant evidence of the close relation between mere literacy and improved farm practices. In fact, the government was frequently criticized for actually hindering the spreading of knowledge. The well-known economist and educator, Professor A. A. Manuilov, wrote in 1905: "The access of peasants to books was hindered to the utmost by the authorities; lectures and talks in the village, even when dealing with strictly specialized subjects, met actually almost insurmountable obstacles." [4] And there was considerable other testimony in a similar vein.

Technical assistance for small farmers was especially needed in a country like Russia with its difficult climatic conditions. It was, and is, a country suffering from frequently recurrent droughts and crop failure, bringing in their wake severe famines that aggravate the agrarian crisis still further. But instead of concentrating on the problem of improving agricultural productivity through general and technical education, and technical and credit assistance to farmers, the government policy and legislation were directed more and more towards increasing the regimentation of the peasant by the mir, and by the bureaucracy. Government policy aimed, in fact, at tightening the legal isolation of the peasantry from the rest of the society and turning it into what an eminent Russian statesman, V. A. Maklakov, called "a kind of caste." [5] I would add, an oppressed caste. All in all, the Tsarist government taught a sort of negative but telling lesson—the lesson of how an agrarian reform should *not* be carried out.

Small wonder that, under such conditions, the peasants saw land shortage as the root of all their difficulties and manifested a strong land hunger. They knew of only one remedy for the low returns from their

[4] A. A. Manuilov, *Pozemel'nyi Vopros v Rossii* [*The Land Question in Russia*] (Moscow, 1905), 47.

[5] V. Maklakov, "The Agrarian Problem in Russia Before the Revolution," *The Russian Review*, 9:3–15 (1950). Reprinted in *The Making of Modern Europe, Book Two: Waterloo to the Atomic Age,* edited by Herman Ausubel (New York, 1951), 881–895.

land; that was to increase their cultivated areas. Plowing up as much of his holding as possible, even at the expense of the scarce meadows and pastures, and without regard to soil erosion, leasing land from the landlords, and, less frequently, purchasing the land at a high price from the landlord or a land speculator—these were the peasant's traditional methods of expanding his crop area. This was, under existing conditions, the path of least resistance. It was easier to continue the same type of farming on a larger area than to reorganize the system of farming on the old holding for which capital and knowledge were lacking.

The leasing of land was particularly widespread. According to estimates of competent authorities, it involved more than one-third of the peasant households. Such leasing increased the total peasant allotted area by roughly a fifth.[6] Fierce competition for leasing land, however, often led to exorbitant rentals. Thus a large number of Russian peasants became, through adversity, part-tenants, part-owners, despite the allotment of land upon Emancipation.

Meantime, the peasant cast covetous eyes upon the estate land. In fact, he never ceased to hope that one day the Tsar would issue another manifesto distributing all estate land to the tillers of the soil. In such a redistribution the Russian peasant saw his real salvation and his mind was impervious to any arguments against it, no matter how sound economically they were. The communal re-partitional system of ownership, with its fluid tenure and egalitarian tendencies, doubtless helped to strengthen this frame of mind. But its historic roots go back to the period of serfdom. The peasants' conception of servitude was often expressed in these words, addressed to the landlords, "We are yours but the land is ours." The peasants' memories harbored many grievances against the landlords, but the reduced holdings that accompanied Emancipation especially rankled as an injustice. This injustice was the more keenly felt because the peasants often had to lease land from their former masters, perhaps the same land that they or their fathers once tilled. It is certainly symptomatic that Lenin, who was a past master in the art of effective exploitation of popular discontent for party ends, insisted, at the turn of the century, on the inclusion in the platform of the then still united (Marxist) Socialist Democratic

[6] V. Bazhaev, "Land Leasing," *Polnaya Entsiklopediya Russkogo Sel'skogo Khozyaistva* [*A Complete Encyclopedia of Russian Agriculture*] (St. Petersburg, 1912), 12:48; N. P. Oganovsky, *Ocherki po Ekonomicheskoi Geografii S.S.S.R.* [*Essays in Economic Geography of the USSR*] (2nd ed., Moscow, 1924), 107.

Party of a somewhat un-Marxist plank for the distribution to the peasants of this so-called cut-off land.

Until the early years of the present century, however, the idea of the new division of estate land, though imbedded in peasant consciousness, did not go beyond rumors and vague expectations. Then the peasant temper changed radically. In 1905, following the weakening of the autocracy as a result of the unsuccessful war with Japan, serious revolutionary disturbances spread from cities to the countryside like wildfire.

To the various socialist parties that had long advocated nationalization or socialization of all land on ideological grounds, the peasant uprising was, of course, so much grist for their mill. But even the moderate liberals, represented in the main by the Constitutional Democratic or Cadet Party, became convinced that the coexistence of large estates and small peasant farmers—an uneasy one since the Emancipation—was no longer tenable. They believed that only the distribution of most of the estate land among the peasants, particularly the land leased by peasants, could allay the violent agrarian unrest that endangered the whole fabric of the Russian state. The moderate liberals therefore strongly advocated distribution of estate land to the peasants who were most in need.

The liberals based their proposals on the legal principle of eminent domain, which permits compulsory acquisition of private property by the state with fair compensation to the owners, when this is dictated by public interest. Emancipation legislation of 1861 was cited as a precedent in this connection. On the economic side, the liberal attitude found support in the generally unprogressive character of Russian estate farming outside the western provinces, where the Polish and German landlords managed their estates with a fairly high degree of efficiency and where agriculture in general had a more intensive character. Elsewhere, landlords found it often more profitable to lease the land to the peasants than to farm it with the aid of hired labor. At best, landlords would employ nearby peasants to work the land with their own implements and horses. This did not bespeak an improved farm technique greatly differing from that prevailing on the peasant land, though higher crop yields per acre were obtained because of the better quality of the estate land.

Thus, Russian estate farming was no *Kulturtraeger* and the socioeconomic losses of its disappearance through an orderly land reform were not considered serious by its liberal proponents. This is a debatable issue, but, in any event, it was not primarily economic considerations but the revolutionary emergency that made the reform urgent in the eyes of the liberals. As Professor Herzenstein, the principal and most persuasive spokesman on the subject for the Cadet Party in the first Russian parliament, put it, "Now we have a conflagration and it must be extinguished. Only an increase in the [peasant] land area can extinguish it." [7]

Bills for distribution of estate land were introduced in the first and second parliaments, or dumas, which the Tsarist government convoked in 1906 and 1907, following the revolution of 1905. The liberal proposals for land reform involved, of course, fair compensation for the owners of estate land that was to be distributed. Such compensation was to be borne partly by the state, partly by the recipient of increased land allotments. The reform proposals also provided for exemptions and safeguards when land distribution would tend to affect production adversely, as, for instance, in cases of valuable industrial crops like sugar beets, grown primarily on estates. Land which had been purchased by the peasants since Emancipation in small plots from the landlords and held in fee simple, as distinguished from the communal "allotted land," was also to be exempt from distribution. Although there were differences of opinion among liberal reformers regarding the form of ownership of estate land to be distributed, there was no question about the continuation of an individual-family type of farming on this land.

It may be appropriate at this point to indicate the statistical relationship between the peasant and estate land. According to the land census of 1905, about 200 million acres of land in European Russia were owned mostly by the nobility and also by the business and professional classes and the imperial family. A little more than half of this area was in less than 10,000 very large estates of over 2,700 acres each. This was the estate land, a large portion of which was proposed for distribution among the peasants. In addition, business corporations and various institutions and churches owned 20 million acres, of which probably only a small part could have been safely distributed. The peasants owned 375 million acres of "allotted" land and, in addition, over 66 million acres purchased from the landlords, or, altogether, in round figures, 440 million acres. To sum up, 130,000 private estates

[7] Speech at the session of May 19, 1906. Reprinted in *Agrarnyi Vopros V Pervoi Gosudarstvennoi Dume* [*The Agrarian Question in the First Parliament*] (Kiev, 1906), 56.

and the imperial family possessed about 200 million acres, or close to half the total holding of 12 million peasant households.[8]

Moderate advocates of land reform realized that distribution of the estates was no panacea, no cure-all for Russia's agrarian ills, but only a first step in the solution of the agrarian problem in Russia. To the conservative opponents who claimed that division of estate land would be a palliative rather than a cure, Professor Kaufman, one of the ablest and most scholarly among the moderate proponents of land reform, replied that when a seriously ill patient is suffering from a high fever it is essential, first of all, to save the patient by breaking the fever before further therapy can be administered.[9] This is precisely what the advocates of moderate land reform sought to accomplish in 1906–07.

To those who feared the detrimental effect of division of estates on agricultural production and on agricultural progress, the advocates of land reform pointed out: 1) that they favored certain safeguards and exemptions; 2) that, in any event, the higher production on estates was due, as I have already mentioned, in no small measure to the better quality of estate land rather than to better technique and larger capital investment; 3) that the large area of estate land leased by peasants on a short-term basis would be farmed no worse, and probably better, when it was in the peasants' permanent possession, and the payment for the land was less than the exorbitant rents formerly charged. Here, especially, the Russian liberals were on strong ground.

Nearly half a century has passed and yet, today, one often hears repeated the same fallacy about the evil effects that land reform will have on production in countries where farm tenancy is even more widespread and more oppressive than it was in Russia. However, it must be further said that the advocates of land reform fully recognized, as the writings and speeches of Kaufman, Herzenstein, Kutler, and other liberal experts and leaders demonstrated, that land redistribution must be accompanied by an all-out effort to raise the technical level of peasant agriculture, to increase production through education and through technical and credit assistance to the peasant farmers. The reformers may have been over-optimistic on what could be thus accom-

[8] Statistical data are from I. V. Chernyshev, *Sel'skoe Khozyaistvo Dovoennoi Rossii i SSSR* [*Agriculture of Prewar Russia and the U.S.S.R.*] (Moscow and Leningrad, 1926), 26, 42–48.

[9] A. A. Kaufman, *Zemlya I Kul'tura. K Voprosy O Zemel'noi Reforme* [*Land and Culture. Concerning the Question of Land Reform*] (Moscow, 1906), 27.

plished. Perhaps they were too strongly influenced by the example of the intensive peasant agriculture in Denmark and other Western European countries and, in that pre-tractor age, were not sufficiently alive to the advantages of large-scale farming on the vast Russian steppes. But they rightly criticized the Government for doing nothing or very little to help the peasants to improve their farming, and then advocating increased production as an alternative to land reform. I do not think it is necessary for me to discuss here the much less realistic, more radical land reform proposals of the socialist parties at the time.

Even the government itself, when the revolutionary disturbances were at their height, toyed with the idea of land reform based on the distribution of estate properties. A bill to this effect was drafted in the winter of 1905–06 by N. N. Kutler, Minister of Agriculture in Count Witte's cabinet. But by the spring of 1906, the government felt that it had a firm grip on the situation, and resolutely turned its back on the division of estates. The Tsarist government succeeded in crushing the revolution in 1906 and the estates were saved for their owners. Herzenstein, who championed the peasants' interests in the parliament, was slain by the "black hundreds"—the precursors of the modern Fascists. There were to be no land reforms of a liberal democratic character. And likewise—and this is highly important—*ipso facto* there was to be no genuine representative constitutional government. For the experience of the first two short-lived parliaments, dissolved by the Tsar, proved conclusively that such a government would be deeply committed to the kind of land reform that was anathema to Tsarism.

Because of this strong link between land reform and genuine constitutionalism, Russia's failure to adopt land reform before the First World War had wide repercussions, and not only in that country alone but far beyond its borders—in the arena of world history, where Russia was destined to play its fateful role. I think it is not a far-fetched speculation to say that the history of the last half century would have been vastly different if Russia had emerged from the turbulence of the early 1900's as an agrarian and political democracy—and it could not become one without becoming the other.

It is true, that the government, under the leadership of Prime Minister Stolypin (1906–1911), carried out its own kind of agrarian reform. Its principal objective was the creation of a relatively small class of strong, independent peasant proprietors, with a firm attachment to the principles of private property and efficient farming. Such a class, it was hoped, would be an ally of large estate owners, and would act as a buffer between them and the mass of small peasant farmers. Stolypin aptly characterized this policy in his classical phrase as the "wager" on the strong elements of the peasantry in preference to the weaker ones. In short, it was to be a sort of counter-revolution to prevent another revolutionary outburst in the village.

In pursuance of its objective the government adopted a number of measures that, despite some faults and reservations, were, on the whole, beneficial to agricultural progress, notably: the ambitious agricultural colonization program in Asiatic Russia; the drive to consolidate the scattered fragmented peasant holdings into single land tracts; the relaxation of restrictions on peasant property and civil rights; and the extension of credit assistance to the peasants for purchases of land from the estate owners who were anxious to dispose of their properties after the revolution of 1905.

However, the keystone of the Stolypin reform was not found in such progressive measures but rather in an attack on the mir, the institution of communal land tenure.[10] Here was a drastic reversal of Tsarist agrarian policy. The protection of the mir was one of the basic tenets of this policy prior to 1906, when this institution was considered a conservative bulwark in the village. Although, paradoxically, a large section of Russian socialists, the Narodniki, who made the mir the alpha and omega of their philosophy, held exactly the opposite view. The revolution of 1905 disillusioned the Tsarist government about the mir's role as guardian of the status quo in the countryside. The government now saw in the mir, with its egalitarian tendencies and its shielding of the economically weak elements of the peasantry, an obstacle to the creation of a class of individual peasant proprietors on whom it could depend.

The mir, therefore, must go, whatever the wishes of the peasant masses. Its fiscal functions were ended with the cancellation of redemption payments in 1907 and the abolition of the collective liability for taxes by 1905. The legislation adopted for this purpose has been described in detail by competent scholars.[11] I think the significance of the Stolypin land legislation was well epitomized by the eminent Russian historian and statesman, Paul Milukov: "Stolypin proposed his

[10] For a more detailed discussion of the mir, see Lazar Volin, "The Peasant Household Under the Mir and the Kolkhoz in Modern Russian History," *The Cultural Approach to History*, edited by Caroline F. Ware for the American Historical Association (New York, 1940), 125–139.

[11] G. T. Robinson, *Rural Russia Under the Old Regime* (New York, 1932), George Pavlovsky, *Agricultural Russia on the Eve of the Revolution* (London, 1930).

own landlord tainted reform in opposition to those democratic proposals which led to the dissolution of the first two Russian parliaments. The Stolypin reform tried to divert peasants from the division of the land of the nobles by the division of their own land for the benefit of the most prosperous part of the peasantry." [12]

Thus the Stolypin reform, though in many respects progressive, lacked the basic appeal to the discontented peasant masses that the liberal proposals for land reform possessed. It could not, therefore, conciliate Russian peasantry, at least not within the short period before another political crisis occurred. I may add here, that both the internal political and the external international situations strongly pointed toward the likelihood of such a crisis.

The estate owners merely won a Pyrrhic victory. As soon as the monarchy was overthrown, in 1917, the agrarian problem again came to the fore as a phoenix rising from its own ashes. The alternatives now were a land reform, sponsored by democratic socialists, still orderly, but more radical in character than in 1906, or an agrarian revolution aided and abetted by Lenin and Company. For Lenin, the orthodox Marxist, a peasant revolution was a temporary opportunistic expedient in the bid for power. For this purpose, he stooped to borrow from the ideological arsenal of his anti-Marxist and peasantophile opponents, the Socialist Revolutionaries.

Speed now was essential to any orderly democratic agrarian reform, but this made its accomplishment that much more difficult under the chaotic conditions prevailing in the summer of 1917. The overthrow of the Kerensky government by the Bolsheviks cleared the path for an agrarian revolution, which actually began in the form of widespread peasant disturbances even before the Bolshevik coup. In the process of wholesale land redistribution, not only the estate system was liquidated, but also the larger peasant holdings, and especially the class of new peasant proprietors created by the Stolypin legislation. For the peasant masses, however, this was also a Pyrrhic victory. In a little more than a decade, they too were dragooned into the state-controlled kolkhozy after a gruesome struggle that took a terrible toll of human life and economic wealth from the Russian countryside. [13] Thus Russia, which had demonstrated the tragic consequences of its failure to carry

[12] Paul Milukov, "A Republic or a Monarchy," *Krestyankaya Rossiya* 4:54 (Prague, 1923).

[13] See Lazar Volin, *A Survey of Soviet Russian Agriculture* (U.S. Department of Agriculture, Monograph 5, Washington, D.C., 1951), 194 pages; Lazar Volin, "Soviet Agricultural Collectivism in Peace and War," *American Economic Review*, (Papers and Proceedings of the 63rd Annual Meeting of the American Economic Association) 41, No. 2, pp. 465–474 (May, 1951).

out a timely democratic land reform, was destined to teach the world still another lesson, namely, the failure of the Communist land reform to create an agrarian order that would be in harmony with the historic aspirations of the peasant masses for land and liberty.

SUGGESTIONS FOR ADDITIONAL READING

Jerome Blum, *Lord and Peasant in Russia from the Ninth to the Nineteenth Century,* Princeton, 1961.

G. A. Pavlovsky, *Agricultural Russia on the Eve of the Revolution,* London, 1930.

Geroid T. Robinson, *Rural Russia Under the Old Regime,* New York, 1932.

COLLECTIVIZATION OF AGRICULTURE IN SOVIET RUSSIA *

Lazar Volin

The Revolution appeased peasant land hunger by dividing and distributing the estates of former landlords, and for about a decade the peasants remained "a citadel of individualism" in a collectivized economy. Eventually, however, theoretical and other considerations dictated their forced collectivization. This process and the resulting weaknesses of the collective system are analyzed by Dr. Volin in the selection that follows.

Agrarian democracy is confronted today with a double challenge: the challenge of the survival of feudal or semifeudal forms of land tenure which provoke agrarian unrest that is cleverly exploited by those twin enemies of democracy, Communism and Fascism, and the challenge of Soviet collectivism.

---

* Reprinted with permission of the copyright owners, the Regents of the University of Wisconsin, from K. H. Parsons, R. J. Penn, and P. M. Raup, eds., *Land Tenure* (The University of Wisconsin Press: 1956), pp. 374–83.

That agrarian collectivism is part and parcel of world Communism in action is not open to doubt. It is no longer confined to the Soviet official frontiers, which themselves have greatly expanded. Since the war, it has been apparent that wherever the Soviet fiat reaches, the kolkhoz, as the Russians call the collective farm, eventually follows as a symbol of the Soviet way of life. Thus, the Russian collectivization experiment is today of more than merely academic or theoretical interest to the free world. It is appropriate, therefore, that a conference such as this should address itself to so serious a challenge.[1]

That collectivization of agriculture has always been the ultimate objective of the Bolsheviks is made abundantly clear by Lenin's writings and by official party literature. The Bolshevik position rests squarely on the Marxist dogma, which has been swallowed by Russian Marxists lock, stock, and barrel ever since the Marxists split off from the older agrarian-minded Russian socialism of the Narodniki or Populists in the 1880's. Central to this dogma is the predilection for bigness arising from the Marx-Engels doctrine of superiority of large-scale production in agriculture as in the manufacturing industry. Both agriculture and industry are envisaged as subject to the same evolutionary law of concentration, uninhibited by the economic law of diminishing returns or the biological factors peculiar to agriculture. Only large-scale farming is capable, according to this view, of applying effectively the results of modern science and technology. And a corollary of all this is the thesis of the eventual disappearance of the small peasant producer.[2]

However, the writings of Marx, and especially of Engels and Lenin, tend to support the view that the Marxist-Leninist ideology does not preclude a gradualist approach to agricultural collectivization. Lenin himself, as is well known, was a great master of compromise in the agrarian sphere. In 1917, he even took over the program of his opponents, the agrarian-minded Socialist Revolutionaries, and championed the rebellious small peasant farmers against the landlords. It was, undoubtedly, this policy of appeasement of the peasants by giving them a green light to divide the estate land which helped the Bolsheviks to consolidate power after they seized it. And herein lies a lesson of

[1] The International Conference on Land Tenure and Related Problems in World Agriculture, Madison, Wisconsin, 1951. [Editor's note.]

[2] See the excellent treatment of the subject by David Mitrany, *Marx Against the Peasant: A Study in Social Dogmatism* (Chapel Hill, North Carolina, 1951). See also Victor Chernov, *Marks i Engel's o Krestyanstve* (Moscow, 1906).

crucial importance for other countries in which the issue of land reform is ripe or over-ripe. For if the democratic Kerensky government
had realized in 1917 that speed was of the essence in the matter of
land reform to which they were committed, the Bolsheviks would have
been deprived of an important advantage in their bid for power—of
posing as defenders of the peasants' interests and their aspirations for
land. The Russian peasants, however, apparently had an early premo-
nition of evil things to come from the Bolshevist regime. This was seen
on the only occasion when the peasants were able to vote as they
pleased; that is, in the relatively free elections to the Constituent Assembly, held soon after the Bolsheviks seized power in November,
1917. In that election the peasants voted overwhelmingly against
Lenin's party and gave a large majority to his opponents, the Socialist
Revolutionaries. Needless to say, the Assembly was speedily dispersed
by the Bolsheviks, who clamored for its convocation when they were
in opposition.

In fact, conflict between the Soviet government and the peasantry
began early. Despite this, the gradualist approach to collectivization
prevailed, with Stalin's approval, until the late twenties. The reasons
for the abandonment of gradualism and for the radical shift of the
Soviet agrarian policy towards speedy collectivization were partly ideological and partly grounded in the economic and political situation of
Soviet Russia. For one thing, the Soviet regime was more strongly entrenched after a decade of existence and could, therefore, follow a
bolder policy than during the earlier years. Nevertheless, the ever-
present suspicion of peasant agriculture as a breeding ground of
capitalism, which might encircle and defeat socialism, or, as I would
prefer to call it, Sovietism in the USSR, persisted. This suspicion was
theoretically inspired by the Marxist dogma and was reflected in Lenin's often-quoted proposition that "small-scale production gives birth
to capitalism and the bourgeoisie constantly, daily, hourly, with ele-
mental force and in vast proportion." Not only small individual farming
but even a peasant in a collective farm cultivating his kitchen garden
of an acre or two is suspect.

Even more important was the ambitious and lopsided industrialization program of the five-year plans. This involved, in the first instance, the development of heavy industry, which again was dictated
by a combination of ideological and politico-military considerations.
Such an industrial expansion required, of course, capital. And where
was the requisite capital to be drawn from when foreign sources were

unavailable, if not largely from agriculture? In an agrarian country like Russia, it was, as Stalin admitted, something of a tribute paid by agriculture on the altar of socialist industrialization in the form of high taxes and the famous "scissors"—the opening of the scissors representing the disparity between the low prices paid by the state for farm products and high prices charged for manufactured goods of the nationalized monopolistic industry.

The peasants naturally resisted such squeezing tactics by refusing to sell their produce to the government, especially when the harvest was poor. On occasion, they even went so far as to curtail production. The net effect was that the propensity of small peasant farming towards self-sufficiency was greatly enhanced by the industrialization policy of the Soviet government—the very policy which urgently required increased production for the market but did not offer sufficient incentives to stimulate the peasants to produce. Let us not forget in this connection that the division of the estates in 1917 also dealt a serious blow to commercial production.

The Soviet leadership, therefore, was confronted, in the late twenties, with a crucial dilemma; either to slow down the tempo and alter the character of industrialization by shifting the emphasis from heavy to light industry producing consumer goods, or to acquire thoroughgoing control of agriculture, which was the last citadel of individualism in the USSR, since all the other important branches of economy were already nationalized. Stalin was bent on "building socialism in one country" and wanted now to out-Trotsky the exiled Trotsky, who advocated a more rapid industrialization and a tougher policy against the peasants. Stalin also became resolved upon rapid industrialization and maximum development of heavy industry. Any deviation from this course he rejected as a "suicide, a blow to our whole industry . . . a retreat from the objective of industrialization of our country and, on the contrary, its transformation into an appendix to the capitalistic economy." However, he conceded that the situation would have been different if Russia was an industrial country like Germany or was not the only country with a "proletariat dictatorship."

With such a firm commitment to "socialist" industrialization, the die was cast for a collectivist solution of the agrarian problem. The collectivization policy was also encouraged by three theoretically attractive ideas which certainly are not inherent in or, with the exception of the machine-tractor stations, peculiar to a collectivist system: (1) The advantage of rapidly consolidating into larger fields the numerous, scattered, noncontiguous strips into which small peasant holdings were usually divided and which were a source of much inefficiency. In this conection it must also be pointed out that as a result of the division and redivision of holdings during the Revolution and post-revolutionary period many uneconomic farm units, lacking draft power and implements, were created. (2) The enthusiasm for the tractor, which . . . fascinated Soviet leaders from Lenin down. The tractor reinforced the Marxist faith in the efficacy of large-scale farming and was to be the spearhead of technical revolution in agriculture. (3) The possibility of maximizing the use of tractors, combines, and other farm machinery by pooling them in state-owned central machine-tractor stations.

I shall not linger here on the gruesome aspects of the forced collectivization and liquidation of the so-called kulaki, or fists. The horrible ordeal of Russian peasants during the frightful thirties, driven into collectives or off the land, must be only too well known to you. Doubtless Marx and Engels, who so eloquently portrayed the hardships of the British factory worker during the Industrial Revolution, and maybe even Lenin, would turn in their graves if they could see the uprooted, starving, suffering humanity in the Russian countryside as the practical consequence of the doctrines they preached. Stalin, it is true, nonchalantly declared in 1929, in regard to the liquidation of the kulaki, that in accordance with the Russian proverb, "once you cut off the head there is no use crying about the hair." But Stalin, also confessed to Winston Churchill, during his wartime visit to Moscow, that the terrible strain of the collectivization struggle with the peasantry exceeded even that of the war.

By the middle 1930's, collectivization became an accomplished fact. Thus the trend towards small peasant farming, which set in with the emancipation of the Russian peasantry from serfdom in the 1860's and which was confirmed by the peasant revolution of 1917/18, was reversed. At a staggering cost, both economic and human, the land and capital of some 20 million small independent peasant farmers were pooled together, with certain exceptions, into some 240,000 collective farms, or kolkhozy. Side by side with these, there were set up about 4,000 relatively large state farms (sovkhozy), owned and operated outright by the government with the aid of hired wage labor. In addition, there were more than 6,000 state machine-tractor stations, servicing the collectives and acting as an important mechanism for extraction of farm products from the collective agriculture. In 1938, 86 per cent of the crop was cultivated by collectives, 9 per cent by state farms, and only 5 per cent was farmed individually, mainly as kitchen-garden holdings of members of collectives.

Just a few words about the salient features of the new collective farms.[3] They are essentially institutions of socialized production, though not all production is socialized. The peasant family also does a little farming of its own. Consumption has remained primarily on an individual or family basis. The peasant families continue to live in their own dwellings in the villages as they did, for the most part, before collectivization. Tractors, combines, and other complicated machinery are owned as a rule not by the collectives but by the state MTS.[*] Thus collectives are divorced from their power-machine base, which is controlled and operated by the state, though they still own the greatly decreased number of horses.

Full-fledged communistic farms, as well as the more simple types of producers' cooperatives for joint cultivation of land organized during earlier stages of collectivization, were banned in favor of what is known as the present artel type of collective. Economic equality in collective farms was tabooed by the levellers of the Kremlin in the interest of productive efficiency. A complicated system of payment by results, resembling a piecework wage, was introduced. There is a steep differentiation of the income of collective farmers according to amount of work and skill required. The growth of a new aristocracy of skilled labor and farm supervisors and managers has been encouraged. No payment is permitted for land or capital contributed by members in present-day collective farms. The collective farmer is a residual claimant to the income of the collective after the obligations to the state for the delivery of farm products, including payments to machine-tractor stations, are met. These deliveries have the first priority, or, as Stalin significantly put it, they constitute the first commandment of the collective farmers. Capital and current production expenses must also be defrayed before any distribution is made to members, except for small

[3] For a more detailed discussion, see Lazar Volin, *A Survey of Soviet Russian Agriculture*, United States Department of Agriculture Monograph No. 5 (Washington, D.C., 1951), Ch. III.

[*] Since this was written the MTS have been abolished, retaining only repair functions. Their tractors and heavy farm machinery have been sold to the kolkhozy. Western observers have attributed this change to the increased production and availability of tractors and the fact that the management of the super-collectives (mentioned later) has indeed been "politically reliable," thus obviating the need for the indirect control formerly exercised by the MTS. [Editor's note.]

advances. Thus the collective farmer bears practically all the risks that the independent farmer does, but, unlike the latter, he has actually no share in the control of the collective enterprise.

It is true that in theory the collective farm is a democratic, self-governing organization, electing its own officers. In practice, however, the collective farms' self-government is largely a fiction. The Bolshevik authorities appoint and remove the officers of collectives at will. In turn, the latter boss the rank-and-file farmers and often manage the finances of the collectives as they please. This situation has not changed, despite incessant fulminations in the Soviet press against the expensive and inefficient collective farm bureaucracy. And, in any event, the collective farms are supposed to function within the orbit of Soviet planned economy. The collectives must fulfill the goals and regulations of the Kremlin planners, which their local agents must enforce at any cost. These goals and regulations, with regard to which the peasants, in practice, have nothing to say, touch nearly every aspect of farm production and distribution. The collective farmer, therefore, lost the degree of independence possessed by the small peasant farmer, but he has not gained the advantages of a regular wage possessed by the Soviet factory worker; nor has he the joy that comes from participation in a genuinely democratic cooperative undertaking, like the cooperative farms in Israel.

By contrast, the Soviet government, which has full power of control over collective farming and is a partner with a first priority to its portion of the output, does not share, or shares little, in the risks. Thus Soviet agrarian collectivism is like a double-faced Janus, looking with one face towards the Communist party state and with the other towards the peasant.

I will pass over quickly the crisis into which collectivization had plunged Russian agriculture in the early thirties. The poorly worked, weedy fields, with consequent low yields per acre and small production of crops, the mounting exactions of the Soviet state, which kept the city worker alive but brought famine to the Russian countryside in which several million people perished, the disastrous decline in livestock numbers, including draft animals, the consequent shortage of draft animal power, which could not be rapidly replaced by tractors, and the detrimental effect of all this on the standard of living of the people of Russia—on their diet, clothing, and footwear—these are the manifestations of the crisis which are probably familiar to all of you.

Confronted with this crisis, the Soviet government proceeded, in the middle thirties, to what was known in Soviet terminology as the "organizational-economic" strengthening of collective farming. Without giving up its grip over Russian agriculture, the government introduced concessions to peasant individualism. These concessions were on a much more limited scale than in 1921, when Lenin introduced the celebrated New Economic Policy, or NEP. Unlimited requisitions of farm products were replaced by a stiff but nonetheless certain tax in kind. Peasants were encouraged to operate on their own an acre or so of land and a few animals in addition to their work on the collective farms. It was a sort of "an acre and a cow" type of farming. With it went also restricted, but by no means unimportant, opportunities to sell part of their produce in the free market at much higher prices than were paid by the government. This "acre and a cow" policy was especially emphasized with the promulgation, in 1935, of the new "model charter," or constitution, of the collective farm. The charter, moreover, aimed at ending the instability of collective landholding. It provides that the tenure of the collectives in the land they occupy is to be permanent, and a title deed is to be issued to each collective farm after proper surveying operations.

Turning now to the question of the size of the farm unit, it is evident that at first no limit was set. The maxim "the larger the better" guided early Soviet collectivization practice. This gigantomania, as later it began to be disparagingly called, is much better recognized in the case of the huge state farms. The average area sown per state grain farm for the 1932 harvest exceeded 11,000 acres, and the total land area per farm at the beginning of that year was more than 37,000 acres. Similar tendencies towards gigantomania, though on a smaller scale, prevailed also in the collectivization of peasant farming.

However, by the mid 1930's, it seemed as if the costly lesson was learned—that hugeness is not synonymous with optimum size or good farm management. At any rate, many of the large state farms were subdivided and some of their land was turned over to collectives.

In the case of collective farms, also, inefficiencies resulting from early unlimited growth began to be recognized. In the first place, the subdivision of collectives into so-called brigades or sections, headed by a brigadier or foreman, was officially emphasized. Each brigade was to include from forty to sixty workers and was to be assigned a separate plot of land for a period of several years, covering a crop rotation cycle, as well as the necessary animal draft power and farm implements. In the late thirties, a smaller operational unit in the collectives, the so-called zveno (literally "link"), or squad, of about a dozen workers came much to the fore. The squads were especially favored by the Soviet authorities for the growing of intensive crops requiring a great deal of labor, such as sugar beets and cotton. But their use in grain farming was also encouraged. These squads were particularly effective in combatting the frequently slipshod work of the MTS. The small squads appeared to have elicited more interest in their work from the collective farmers than did the larger brigades.

Subdivision of large collectives also was not uncommon in the 1930's. For example, four large collectives in the Spassk district of Ryazan province in central Russia were each divided into two. On the other hand, the very small collective farms in the northern and north-central regions were long considered inefficient, and "voluntary" merger of such collectives was officially "recommended." But it should be noted that the character of the terrain itself in the northern and north-central regions, criss-crossed by forests, lakes, marshes, etc., militated against large farms, just as the level, more uniform terrain favored large farms in the southern and eastern steppes. Be that as it may, in the north the average size of the collective farm was increasing in the middle thirties, while in the south and east it was decreasing. In general, however, such subdivision and mergers of collective farms as took place before the war were proceeding in a quiet, orderly manner, without the usual fanfare of a drive or campaign so characteristic of the Soviet organizational methods.

The restricted concessions to peasants and the end of gigantomania contributed greatly to such recovery as took place in Soviet agricultural production after the severe underproduction crisis. Increased mechanical equipment and improved farm practices and attention to yields per acre also helped. However, this recovery was too limited in the face of the rapidly growing population to make the early Bolshevik promises of a more abundant life for the masses a reality. But the Soviet government was able to acquire cheaply increasing supplies of farm products, and this greatly facilitated its super-industrialization program with all its waste and inefficiency. The flow of surplus manpower from collectivized agriculture to industry also contributed to its development.

The phase of limited concessions to appease the peasants ended in the late 1930's. The pendulum of Soviet agrarian policy again took a sharp swing towards intensified collectivism. The tax in kind was increased by changing the basis of assessment from the crop area, specified by the government plan, to the total or arable land of a collective. Measures were also taken for the building up of communal or collectivized livestock which, as could be expected, proved to be the Achilles' heel of collective farming. But the government's effort principally centered on the curbing of personal farming on their own small plots by the collective farmers, who, incidentally, owned most of the livestock except horses.

In theory, of course, the personal farming of the collectivized peasants is supposed to have a strictly supplementary character, subsidiary to the basic economy of the collective farm. In practice, however, personal farming has played a much more important role in the economic welfare of the peasants in collective farms. It has also proved a thorn in the side of the Kremlin. Such personal farming creates an economic dualism in the collective that can and does result in competition and conflict between the collectivist and the individualist elements, which the present artel organization of collective farming is supposed to reconcile.

Frequent complaints have been made by Soviet spokesmen that the peasants, particularly women, cultivate these little plots most intensively to the neglect of collective fields. This is especially true when the returns from collective farms are small—and they have often been very small. But it is a sort of vicious circle. For the very preoccupation of the peasant with personal farming has frequently tended to keep the collective farm returns small.*

Of course, it is not the addition of a few hundred thousand acres to the several hundred million acres of collective land that is coveted by the Kremlin. It is, rather, the peasant labor employed on the personal plots and the example it may set of poor collective discipline. With smaller personal plots, more of the peasant's time should be available for work on the collective farm. He is likely to become a more compliant worker, more akin to the factory proletariat. Likewise the development of collectivized (communal) animal husbandry at the expense of individually owned livestock, an objective relentlessly pursued by the Soviet government, helps the process of conversion of the peasant farmer into an agricultural laborer.

The wartime decline in collective agricultural production and the existence of considerable untilled land provided an opportunity for again extending personal farming by collective farmers, which was tolerated by the government. But since 1946 the government has called

---

* As recently as 1959, the private plots representing about 2 per cent of the usable land area were accounting for approximately 25 per cent of total agricultural production. [Editor's note.]

a halt to this temporary leniency and reverted to the stringent collectivist policy pursued before the war. Until 1950, however, there were no significant departures from the prewar pattern of Soviet agrarian collectivism. But during that year a new phenomenon leading to what, perhaps, may be best designated as super-collectivism came to the fore.[4]

The first bombshell was an unsigned article in *Pravda* of February 19, 1950. It severely criticized the member of the Politburo and Chairman of the Council for Kolkhoz Affairs, Andreev, who was long the Kremlin's authoritative spokesman on agricultural policy. Andreev was accused of championing the widespread use of the zveno (the squad) in preference to the large unit, the brigade. The article entirely overlooks the numerous claims made in Soviet publications that the crops received much better care under the zveno system, with favorable effects on yields. Immediately following the publication of the article, a campaign was started in the Soviet press, extolling the brigade and condemning the formerly much-favored zveno. Incidentally, Andreev characteristically "confessed" publicly to his errors a few days after the critical *Pravda* article. More, however, was to come in the way of gigantomania.

Sporadic reports of collective farm mergers, which had a suspicious ring, began to appear in the Soviet press late in 1949. But on March 7, 1950, another member of the Politburo and the new Moscow party boss, Khrushchev, made an "election" speech which was the opening gun in a far-reaching collective farm merger campaign.

The merger campaign apparently began in the Moscow province, which served as a sort of geographic spearhead. However, it was not confined to any particular locality but spread far and wide over the whole Soviet Union from the Baltic to the Pacific and from the Arctic to the Black Sea. Regions where farms were large were affected equally with those where they were small.

It was stated by the Minister of Agriculture, Benediktov, in March, 1951, that the number of collective farms during 1950 decreased from 252,000 to 123,000. More than two-thirds of all collectives were merged into 60,000 large super-collective farms. The number of collectives merged in the new consolidated farms varied from two to fourteen. Mergers involving seven to nine collectives were not uncommon. However, as Khrushchev pointed out, many of the mergers were effected

---

[4] The discussion from this point on follows in the main the author's article "The Turn of the Screw in Soviet Agriculture," *Foreign Affairs*, XXX (1952), 279–88.

only "legally," i.e., administratively, and actual unification was still to be carried out.

The phase of the merger campaign which created perhaps the most furor was the prospective large-scale resettlement of the rural population. A strong impression was given by official speeches and press reports that the merger of collectives was also to be accompanied by the integration of numerous villages into a smaller number of larger settlements, sometimes called agro-towns (agro-gorod). However, this very soon became a dead issue.

In speeches and articles dealing with the theme of farm consolidation, Khrushchev and other Soviet spokesmen painted an attractive picture of the supposed advantages and benefits of large collective farms as compared with smaller units. It is doubtful, however, whether the technical advantages of large-scale farming really weighed so heavily in the merger campaign. For, as was pointed out earlier, this campaign has not confined itself only to the consolidation of small collectives. Farms which everywhere outside the USSR would be considered as large were affected as well.

Much was made, for instance, of the consolidation of the relatively small fields to facilitate tractor operations. But this will be difficult to carry out precisely in the small collectives of the northern and central regions where it would be most advantageous. Here, as was pointed out earlier, small tracts of tillable land are dotted with forests, lakes, and marshes. In general, the rapid, indiscriminate farm mergers, without regard to the wide regional variations in topographical, soil, and climatic conditions, or types of farming in so large a country as Soviet Russia, suggest strongly that the central objective of this policy is not primarily to secure greater efficiency in the combination and use of various factors of production. Of course, there are probably some instances in which mergers of two or more collectives may be conducive to more efficient operation. But it is a far cry from this to the reviving of the gigantomania of the early 1930's, which was officially and repeatedly condemned as detrimental to efficiency.

What, then, was the rationale of the merger drive? It is symptomatic that Khrushchev stressed the key role of managers in the consolidated farms and the necessity of paying them higher salaries. After the merger campaign was under way, much was made in the Soviet press of the consolidated Communist party organizations in the merged collectives. In this manner the relative importance of the Communists and the Communist control mechanism is enhanced in the new super-collectives.

It can be gathered from these and many other clues that an ironclad government control of collectives has been a powerful motive behind the merger drive. The smaller the number of collectives, the easier it is to find managers who are not only efficient but also politically reliable from the Soviet point of view and will zealously deliver the prescribed quotas of farm products. Furthermore, while the elective character of the management in the collectives had already been largely a formality before the merger campaign, it is likely to become even more so. The gap between the new management of the large consolidated collective farms and the rank and file is likely to grow. Such a depersonalization of management is very important from the Soviet standpoint since it tends to increase the driving power of the managers and, *ipso facto*, to tighten the labor discipline in collectives.

Thus, the merger of farms into super-collectives should enable the government to exercise stricter controls. This conforms to the generally more collectivist trend of the Soviet agrarian policy since the late thirties, which was only temporarily relaxed during the war. What is more important, the tightening of control is closely linked with the central objective of Soviet agrarian policy, namely the maximizing of agricultural production and especially of government procurements of farm products. For the Kremlin has been confronted with rather slow postwar recovery of agriculture, and this in the face of growing numbers of mouths to feed and the intensive preparation for war, in which food plays so signal a role. In order to increase production, it was natural for the Bolsheviks to resort to ruthless driving of farm labor into the consolidated collectives, rather than to rely on increased economic incentives to farmers. Such incentives would have to be in terms of consumer goods, which are in short supply, due largely to the emphasis on armament. The shortages of manpower and draft power since the war, which require increased exertion of the available labor force on the farms, probably also contributed to the decision to buttress the collective farm management.

The merger of collectives also provided new opportunities for limitation of personal farming carried on by collective farmers, which should make more labor available for collective work. There are indications that when several collective farms were merged, the size of each member's personal plot was often scaled down to the level of the collective with the smallest plots. Statements in the Soviet press in 1951 criticized the reduction of the plots, but it may well be a case of locking the barn after the horse is stolen.

Much, no doubt, remains to be done to implement consolidation, even from an administrative standpoint, let alone the more technical aspects. The selection of new managers for the super-collective farms has not proven an easy task. Even more time will be required for such matters as the consolidation of collective fields, building of new farm centers, etc.

As a matter of fact, the super-collective farm may well prove, as did its predecessors in the early thirties, too unwieldy to manage. Should the Kremlin become convinced of this, it would probably not hesitate to jettison the super-collectives, to redivide them. At least, this is the lesson of past Soviet experience. Furthermore, the whole scheme of super-collective farming is predicated on the continued submission of the Russian peasant to the increasing stringency of Soviet regimentation.

That there is a reservoir of smoldering peasant unrest in Russia is hardly doubted by anyone at all familiar with Russian history and contemporary agrarian conditions. Every tightening of the collectivist screw is bound to increase agrarian discontent. The farm merger is certainly in this class. The Kremlin, however, has usually exhibited sufficient elasticity in opening the safety valve of peasant appeasement just enough to prevent an explosion; but as soon as the danger passes, the collectivist offensive is resumed. This has occurred on the Soviet scene in every decade.

Should the new agrarian offensive appear to affect the peasant morale too adversely, it is probable that the Kremlin will make another of its famous zigzags and the gigantomania trend represented by the super-collectives may be reversed. After all, strategic retreats are no novelty to the Bolsheviks, who were taught by Lenin that the road to their goals is often not a straight road, but more like a mountain path with many twists and turns.

On the other hand, there has been some speculation that the merger movement may be brought to its logical conclusion in a complete integration of collective peasant agriculture with state farming into a single "socialist" type, patterned essentially on the state farm. It is argued that the trend towards growing operational control of the collectives by the government and the increase in their size, as a result of the mergers, as well as ideological considerations, dictate their eventual assimilation in such a unified system. Perhaps such an amalgamation may occur eventually.

During the next few years, however, it is doubtful whether the Kremlin would be willing to substitute the regular wage payment for labor prevailing in the state farms for the method under which members of the collective are merely residual claimants to its income. The collective farm method of payment is much more profitable to the Soviet government. And so long as this is the case, it is probable that the fiction of self-government and separate existence of collective and state farms will be maintained.

The famous historical economist Gustav Schmoller stated that "from 1500 to 1850 the great social question of the day in Europe was the peasant question." [5] But in Western Europe, the peasant question as a social problem was largely settled by the French Revolution and the agrarian reforms which were inspired by it, in harmony with the historic aspirations of the people who till the soil. In Russia, however, the peasant question cannot be considered solved as yet by collectivization, which was not spontaneous but imposed on the peasantry by force from above. Compulsory collectivization certainly is not in accord with the Russian peasant's age-long yearning for land and independence. Nor has collectivization brought the peasant masses an improved standard of living; often it has brought the contrary. And this strengthens the belief that the challenge of Soviet collectivism to agrarian democracy is really less formidable than it may appear on the surface.

SUGGESTIONS FOR ADDITIONAL READING

Fedor Belov, *The History of a Soviet Collective Farm*, New York, 1955.
Naum Jasny, *The Socialized Agriculture of the U.S.S.R.*, Stanford, 1949.

TWO VILLAGE SKETCHES *

Gordon Wright

These political profiles of two very different agricultural communities show some of the old and new social forces at work in the French countryside and suggest that more change may be in the offing there. The reader will also get an interesting glimpse of the complexities of the peasant problem and the diversity of France's agrarian structure. Gordon Wright is Professor of History at Stanford University.

[5] Gustav Schmoller, "Grundriss der Allgemeinen," *Volkswirtschaftslehre*, I (1900), 520. Quoted in J. H. Clapham, *The Economic Development of France and Germany, 1815–1914* (Cambridge, 1921), p. 1.

* Reprinted from *Rural Revolution in France: The Peasantry in the Twentieth Century* by Gordon Wright with the permission of the publishers, Stanford University Press. © 1964 by the Board of Trustees of the Leland Stanford Junior University.

Midway between Paris and the Belgian frontier, nestled in a small valley in the heart of the Soissons plateau, lies the hamlet of Epagny. The region has long been one of the principal breadbaskets of France; the plateau's rich soil produces grain crops that would be the envy of the American West. Many of its farms (gigantic by French standards) are highly mechanized, thoroughly modern, and remarkably prosperous. Epagny's 320 inhabitants are isolated from railways and main roads; those who want to visit the metropolis of Soissons must walk a mile to catch the once-a-day bus. Yet they live in relative comfort, thanks to the fact that Epagny was blown to bits during the First World War. No house is more than forty years old, and most houses are miraculously equipped with electricity and running water. Such *confort moderne* is rare indeed in rural France.

Nevertheless, the commune has steadily lost population during the past few decades. Mechanization is partly responsible; it has reduced the demand for labor. But far more important, the young people of Epagny rebel against life in the village. Leisure-time diversion is almost nonexistent; so is opportunity for the future. Three-quarters of the children migrate to the towns or cities as soon as their schooling is over. As a community in the organic sense, Epagny is dying.

Epagny's social structure could scarcely be reduced to simpler terms. In 1950, the business community consisted of a harness maker, a blacksmith, a grocer, and a tavernkeeper. There were five retired persons who had come home to spend their declining years. A priest from a neighboring village passed weekly to say Mass. Beyond this, there were landowners and farm laborers: nobody else.

A closer look at this solidly agricultural community shows at once that it violates all the usual generalizations about France, the nation of smallholders. There are only four farms in the entire commune. Three of them are giants, ranging from 600 to 800 acres each; the fourth is a pygmy of 35 acres. The de Fay family, whose aristocratic forebears have long inhabited the region, controls two of the large farms. The rest of the adult population is made up of farm laborers—mostly native Frenchmen, with a considerable minority of Poles. Here, then, is an example of large-scale capitalistic agriculture tinged with feudal survivals.

Immediately after the Second World War, when Charles de Gaulle's provisional government restored free elections, Epagny shifted to the extreme left in brutal fashion. In 1945, 45 per cent of the voters who went to the polls chose the Communist ticket; in 1946 (when two elections occurred), it was 59 and 60 per cent; in 1951, 61 per cent;

in 1956, 55 per cent. The parties of the moderate left and center were virtually wiped out; only the rightist Independent-Peasant bloc survived as a feeble counterpoise to Communism.

Communism's postwar success in Epagny was all the more striking because the movement was so new there. During the Third Republic, Communist candidates had rarely received a single vote; it was the Socialists, rather, who had swept the polls. Back as far as 1914, a Socialist spellbinder had launched the trend when he told these landless workers: "It's easy to know the right way to vote; just see what the boss does, then vote the opposite way." For the next twenty-five years, Socialism had seemed sufficiently opposite to express the workers' discontent. After 1945, it dwindled to near-extinction; the Socialist ticket got only four votes in 1951. Here, it would seem, was a simple case of a proletarianized farm population that gradually became ripe for revolutionary action, and that finally took the natural step from herbivorous to carnivorous Marxism.

Yet the story is not all told. What of the social relationships in the village as the Red tide rose? Prior to 1940, the big landlords had always controlled the local political machinery of the commune. Jean de Fay was mayor in that era; his son Pierre sat on the town council; the third of the big owners, M. Ancellin, was assistant mayor. Municipal elections in 1945 gave the workers their chance to take over the town hall. But the balloting produced astounding results. The voters chose a town council consisting of seven conservatives and three Socialists, without a Communist in the lot; and the council promptly chose Pierre de Fay as mayor, with Ancellin back in his old post as assistant. During the years that followed, the conservatives' grip on the municipality was never challenged. In 1947, Pierre de Fay led the field with 126 of 130 votes cast; his brother Jean followed with 118; Ancellin got 92. When the Fourth Republic gave way to the Fifth in 1958, de Fay and Ancellin stayed on in their perpetual posts in the town hall.

Here is clear enough evidence that the farm workers of Epagny, however discontented they may be, fall somewhat short of fire-eating class-consciousness. How can it be that these proletarians, who persistently support the Communist ticket in national elections, remain loyal to a landowning aristocrat like de Fay? Most of them will answer that question candidly. "He's not like most of the big shots; he's a *chic type*. And besides, who else around here could be mayor?" Who else, indeed? Most of the able young men go off to the cities, leaving the "rejects" to work on the farms. And when a spark of leadership does appear in some farm laborer, it has precious little chance to develop. Workers who develop political ambitions in villages like Epagny have rarely been able to win the votes of their jealous neighbors. "Why should I vote for Jacques? I'm as good a man as he is."

The fact that peasant Communism exists in a village like Epagny needs little explaining. What is curious here is its flabbiness, its lack of intensity; for these proletarians seem made to order for the Leninist formulas. Some day, perhaps, Epagny may furnish troops for a Communist revolution. It is unlikely ever to furnish leaders.

. . . .

The village of Teillé lies on the southern edge of Brittany, in the pleasant grazing country not far from Nantes. The village postmaster, with a touch of pride, points the way to the farm of Bernard Lambert, second-youngest deputy in the French parliament.

This is a region where feudalism, if it died a legal death in 1789, has survived in spirit and mores right down into our own day. Much of the land was sharecropped until 1945; landowners might drop in unannounced to look over the harvest, to see what was cooking in the kitchen, to take home a chicken from the poultry yard. Some of the older peasants still bow and scrape at such a visit, and greet the landlord as "Monsieur not' maître." Bernard Lambert recalls that in 1938 his father, a *métayer*, won a radio in a raffle—the first set in Teillé, the wonder and delight of the whole village. Two days later the landlord appeared: "Lambert, you owe me money. No luxuries for you while you're in debt. I'll take the radio and credit it to your account." "A good way to make Communists," remarks the younger Lambert dryly.

In politics, the old aristocrats have kept a powerful grip on the region; boxcar names are common in the departmental council, and they often go to parliament as well. After the turn of the century the old elite was challenged by the bourgeois Radical Socialists, who found enough support in the cities and towns to elect a few deputies. Neither Christian Democracy nor Marxism ever made much headway in the area. Here was a classic example of the old rural pattern: on the one side, aristocrats, church, and peasantry; on the other, the anticlerical bourgeoisie.

Lambert was an early rebel against this pattern; he rejected it at the age of twelve. Until then, he had taken for granted his role as a share tenant's son and an obedient Catholic; the priest, he recalls, turned him into a good royalist and even, for a time, into "un petit Pétainiste." Then something opened his eyes (as he now puts it); in 1942 he abruptly stopped going to Mass—abruptly, and permanently.

Yet the breach was never complete on either side; after the war, when a new priest founded a local chapter of the JAC,[1] Lambert was welcomed as a member even though he refused to return to the fold. Here Lambert got his first chance to discuss questions of agronomy, economics, politics, in an atmosphere of remarkable freedom. He read voraciously, discovered that he possessed a natural articulateness of speech, was drawn (like Michel Debatisse) into regional and then national positions of leadership in the JAC. Meanwhile he and a few young neighbors took to working their small rented farms conjointly, and founded a small cooperative slaughterhouse to buck the powerful cattle-dealers' monopoly. They next moved in on their elders who had run the regional farmers' syndicate, and took over complete control. Within a year, the average age of the syndicate's regional governing body dropped from sixty-three to thirty. Their butchering cooperative, harassed by the angry cattle-dealers who controlled all marketing outlets, managed to survive by creating its own markets in cities like Nantes, where it arranged for direct sales to organized consumer groups and trade unions.

After the fall of the Fourth Republic in 1958, de Gaulle convoked the electorate to choose a new National Assembly. Four candidates turned up in the district: an aristocrat, a Radical Socialist, a Poujadist (something new in these parts), and the customary Communist railway employee, who ran for the record. The Radical candidate, André Morice, appeared unbeatable; he had sat in parliament for more than a decade, had recently served as Minister of War, and was generally regarded as a front-runner for the premiership. A wealthy Nantes contractor, he was assured of the bourgeois vote by his social role and his Radical label. But he had kept his fences mended on the right, too, and had recently proved his broadmindedness by supporting the clericals on a school bill. No one in France seemed a surer bet for re-election.

Morice made only one mistake: he challenged the local young farmers' group. A few days before the campaign began, he publicly denounced the organizers of the cooperative slaughterhouse, accusing them not only of pinko leanings but of financial dishonesty as well. The young fire-eaters who were now in control of the regional farmers' syndicate were outraged. Morice, they agreed, must be taught a lesson. But how? At the end of an all-night meeting, they decided to enter a peasant candidate, and to draft Bernard Lambert as their champion.

---

[1] *Jeunesse Agricole Chrétienne.* [Editor's note.]

Lambert himself took no part in the discussion; he was just back from two years as a sergeant in Algeria, fighting a war in which he did not believe and winning a decoration for valor in the process. When a delegation waited on him the next day, he was astounded, and tried to beg off: "I'm just back from the war, I'm in debt, I'm too young, and what do I know about politics anyway?" They persuaded him to think it over for a week, got up a petition signed by a thousand young peasants of the region, and, in the end, won his consent.

The story of that campaign is like something out of Horatio Alger. Everybody who counted lined up behind either Morice or the aristocratic candidate: the well-born, the business group, the prefect and subprefect (whose careers Morice could presumably further), the cattle-dealers to a man, all the important members of the clergy. Back of Lambert there was nobody except a horde of young peasants and a considerable number of young priests, who virtually deserted their farms and flocks for a month to cultivate the district politically. At the end of the first day of balloting, Lambert and Morice were neck and neck; the others lagged far behind. The aristocrat promptly withdrew and threw his support to Morice; for the first time in local memory, the Blue and the Black joined in a solid bloc. The young peasant phalanx, undiscouraged, flung itself into a week of day-and-night action—and the miracle was accomplished. When the runoff ballots were totaled, the count stood 19,636 for Lambert, and 19,229 for Morice.

The manner of Lambert's election was no more unorthodox than his subsequent political behavior in the National Assembly. During his first years as a deputy, he violated virtually every taboo of French politics. He outraged the nationalists by calling for a negotiated peace in Algeria. He voted to end the peasants' ancient privilege of home distillation of alcohol—an act of courage rarely performed by any rural deputy in history. He asserted quite openly that his own party, the Catholic MRP, ought to be liquidated as soon as possible, since Catholics ought not to isolate themselves in a confessional party. He proposed the creation of a state agency that would regularly buy up all farm land that came on the market, with a view to leasing it to small peasants for cooperative cultivation. "The myth of peasant land ownership," he contends, "has bankrupted the peasants; since 1789 they have bought all the land in France three times over." Lambert and his friends have pioneered in an unprecedented kind of farmer-labor action in their region of southern Brittany: the farmers' syndicate and the trade unions there frequently join forces to push their common aims, and to engage in joint demonstrations. Even the Communist-controlled labor movement, the CGT, participates in this common action. "Why not?" asks Lambert. "After all, there are only two things wrong with the Communists—they're too sectarian and too conservative."

Only a miracle, perhaps, could have permitted such a maverick to survive long in politics. When de Gaulle and the National Assembly locked horns in 1962 over the issue of constitutional revision, Lambert joined those who voted for a motion of censure against de Gaulle's Premier. Along with many other young farm syndicalist leaders, Lambert shared de Gaulle's desire for a reinforced presidency, but objected to de Gaulle's indifference to constitutional procedures in achieving that end. The Gaullists did not forgive such lèse-majesté. In the elections that followed, all factions except the Communists joined forces behind a single anti-Lambert candidate of the moderate right. Before this solid coalition of conservatives, Radicals, and Gaullists, Lambert went down to defeat by a vote of 18,512 to 15,306 (with another 2,310 votes wasted on the Communist candidate). Lambert's friends consoled themselves by reflecting that his total vote at the first ballot exceeded that of 1958, and that his old rival André Morice, putting discretion ahead of valor, had chosen not to risk a second defeat.

Perhaps Lambert's brief political career was no more than a spectacular accident. Yet possibly it was more than that: a harbinger of new forces at work in French society, of new ideas and mores, of a kind of grass-roots political action that France has never known before. Perhaps even the radicalism of tomorrow will find its home in the countryside rather than in the cities. As the journalist Jacques Fauvet puts it, "While the world of labor grows less and less revolutionary, the peasant world grows less and less conservative." The locus classicus is as always Tocqueville, who remarked a century ago, "The peasants are the last of all to rise, but they are also the last to sit down."

SUGGESTIONS FOR ADDITIONAL READING

Jacques Fauvet and Henri Mendras, eds., Les paysans et la politique, Paris, 1958.

Henri Mendras, Sociologie de la campagne française, Paris, 1959.

Laurence Wylie, "Social Change at the Grass Roots," Stanley Hoffman et al., In Search of France (Cambridge, Mass., 1963).

GLOSSARY

arable, adj. Suitable for cultivation. Commonly, *arable fields, the arable* refer to land under crops as opposed to pasture; *arable farming,* the growing of grain and root crops.

artificial meadows. Term used for lands on which grasses are grown as opposed to lands (*meadows*) which support grass naturally. Thus also *artificial grasses.*

common, commons. A joint pasture to which all members of a community have a right of access for their livestock.

common rights, communal rights, right of common. Legal right of the members of a community to the use of one another's land. Thus the *right of common pasture* includes the right to graze livestock on the **stubble fields** and the **fallow** as well as on the **commons.** Other examples of *common rights* are gleaning in the fields and vineyards and gathering branches in the forest.

corn. Cereal crops; wheat, rye, etc.

cottager. Commonly, an unattached agricultural worker selling his labor for a specific job or time and deriving part of his subsistence from his cottage garden.

cottar, cotter. Laborer occupying a cottage and garden belonging to a farm and working as a farm servant when required.

drill, v. To plant seed in furrows or rows.

drill. Implement or machinery for this purpose. Also the furrow in which the seed is planted.

enclose, v. To fence off, usually by hedges or stone walls, hitherto **open fields** or **commons,** thus abolishing (or sometimes restricting) the **common rights** enjoyed thereon.

engross, v. To combine two or more farms into one for occupancy by a single owner or tenant.

extensive agriculture. Farming, usually involving a broad acreage, where a relatively light expenditure of labor and working capital per acre is used. Sheep raising and cereal growing are examples.

the fallow, fallow field. Ground ploughed but left unseeded for a year or more to rest the soil. *Fallowing;* the practice of same.

fodder. Food for livestock.

forage. Grasses used as food for livestock, as in grazing, or cut and dried as in hay.

foraging rights. Synonymous with right of common pasture. See **common rights.**

freeholder. By the seventeenth century, a person holding his land in substantially free possession (i.e., unencumbered by any customary servitudes, etc.). Commonly synonymous with *yeomanry.*

horticulture. The cultivation of vegetables and fruit.

husbandry. Synonym for farming; more commonly used in the eighteenth and nineteenth centuries when it had a connotation of skill or art.

intensive agriculture. Farming, usually on smaller plots, in which there is a relatively heavy expenditure of labor and working capital per acre. Dairying, viticulture, vegetable and fruit growing are examples.

ley, leys. Field or fields laid down to grass.

open fields, open-field villages, open-field system. Communal agriculture whereby strips belonging to or worked by individuals were intermixed on unenclosed land, subject to **common rights.** The land was also subject to collective restraints involving the type of crops planted and the time of plowing, harvesting, etc.

pulses. Peas, beans, lentils, etc.

quicksets. Commonly, cuttings of shrubs set in the ground to grow hedges for enclosure.

roots, root-crops. Plants with a fleshy, edible root; in the seventeenth and eighteenth centuries, chiefly turnips used as **fodder.**

rotation. An ordered sequence of different crops on a given piece of land to avoid soil exhaustion. A common early *three-course rotation* would be winter corn (wheat or rye) the first year, spring corn (oats or barley) the second, and in the third year the field would be left **fallow.** Later, where **fallowing** went out of use, a common *four-course rotation* would be peas, wheat, barley, and oats.

specialized agriculture. Farming where the principal activity is the cultivation of one type of crop, as opposed to *subsistence farming*.

stubble field. Field from which grain or grass crops have been harvested. The lower part of the stalks, or remaining *stubble,* is grazed by livestock.

three-field system. System whereby the strips or fields of a manor or domain would be divided into three great sectors for following a **three-course rotation.** It represented an advance over the *two-field system* where one-half the land would lie **fallow** every year.

till, v. To cultivate the soil with plow, harrow, or by manuring, etc.

tillage. Often used as a synonym for **the arable.** Also means the act or condition of being *tilled*.

tilth. Soil or condition of soil after cultivation.

waste, wastes, wasteland. Land unsuitable for cultivation in its unimproved condition (i.e., uncleared or undrained) .

white crops. Wheat, barley, rye, oats.

PB-43840
8